TRAIN CRASH AT
CRUSH
TEXAS

AMERICA'S DEADLIEST PUBLICITY STUNT

MIKE COX

THE
History
PRESS

Published by The History Press
Charleston, SC
www.historypress.com

CONTENTS

PREFACE

T he golden era of passenger train service belonged to my grandparents and, to a lesser extent, my mother and dad, not me. As a baby boomer growing up in the 1950s and early 1960s, I only rode on a pre-Amtrak passenger train twice. The first time was on the Missouri, Kansas and Texas (the Katy), from Denton to Fort Worth, when I was in the second grade and my class was studying transportation. And in the summer of 1970, I took one of the final runs of the Missouri Pacific's Texas Eagle from Austin to San Antonio. Since then, I have made several pleasant trips on Amtrak trains, as well as on trains in the United Kingdom. The result is that I have really come to appreciate trains over planes (and airport security checks) if I have the time and there's a rail connection available. In fact, if rail service existed between Dallas, Houston and San Antonio, I'd never drive to either of those cities again.

Despite my limited experience on passenger trains that were not federally subsidized, from what I have read about the good old days of rail travel and premier passenger trains like the Katy Flyer, the Bluebonnet Special and the Texas Special, I miss them even though they were before my time. When I was in junior high school, the sole surviving MKT passenger train connecting Dallas–Fort Worth to San Antonio via Austin rolled past my school each day. Seeing that train, I wished I could have been sitting in it rather than in my non–air conditioned classroom. Even though by then traditional rail passenger service was near its end, the Katy's streamlined orange and yellow diesel locomotive and shiny passenger coaches rumbling by fueled my daydreams and therefore contributed to my lack of prowess in math.

I first learned of the Crash at Crush in September 1962 when as a seventh grader I read a feature article on the event published in the *Austin American-Statesman*. I have been interested in the quirky story ever since, but I want to thank History Press acquisition editor Ben Gibson for suggesting that I do a book on the Katy's wacky PR stunt of September 15, 1896, and its catastrophic outcome. As I delved into the incident and its background, I found that the story was much more interesting and far broader in scope than I had thought. It is a national story, with a playbill of compelling characters ranging from an innovative scoundrel in Chicago who became a millionaire (not to mention being a bigamist) to a farmer from Iowa who devoted most of his career to staging train wrecks for other people's fun and his profit. In telling this story, I was able to explore the history of the MKT and its influence on the development of the Southwest, the not-so-gay 1890s and the time when railroads and their steam-powered "iron monsters" drove the nation's economy.

The folks who helped with my research for this book might not fill all the seats on a passenger coach, but I'm indebted to a fair number of people.

A special toot of the whistle for old friend Ben Sargent, former *Austin American-Statesman* colleague and winner of a Pulitzer Prize for his editorial cartoons. A longtime railroad buff who's also a qualified locomotive fireman and conductor who volunteers on Austin Steam Train Association runs, he graciously agreed to read my manuscript and was able to switch me to the right track on several technical issues. He also prepared the excellent map of McLennan County in 1896 that shows the location of the crash.

The volunteers at the museum in West, Texas—the nearest community to the site of the Crush smashup—were particularly helpful as I first began my research. It was at the museum where Patricia Cloud told me the story about her grandfather John Foit that I use to open this book. Later that afternoon, she led me to the site of the crash.

Roy Jackson, who runs the Red River Railroad Museum in Denison, Texas (once a major Katy hub), shared all he had on the Crash at Crush and also assisted me with some specific research.

Temple, Texas writer-historian Patty Benoit was a lot of help during my research into ragtime musician Scott Joplin's time in Central Texas and was kind enough to give that chapter a read for accuracy.

The largest collection of archival material related to the crash is held by the Texas Collection at Baylor University in Waco. There Benna Vaughan, Amie Oliver and Geoff Hunt were most helpful. Also in Waco, the nearest large city to the crash site, McLennan County archivist Kerry McGuire helped me locate the court records dealing with the legal aftermath of the staged collision and diligently tried to find other county records concerning the event. (Alas, there are none extant.)

The Katy Railroad Historical Society (www.katyrailroad.org) has done much to collect and preserve the spotty surviving records bearing on the line's colorful history, to capture the recollections of company old-timers and to locate vintage Katy-related photographs. This book greatly benefited from the group's efforts, particularly its digitization of all extant back issues of the *MKT Employee Magazine*. The society also publishes an excellent quarterly magazine, the *Katy Flyer*, featuring well-researched articles on various aspects of the MKT's history, personnel, facilities and rolling stock.

Retired judge Rick Miller of Copperas Cove, Texas, one of the nation's most respected experts on Old West outlaws, mailed a packet of information he ran down for me.

Rusty Williams of Dallas, a writer and fellow recovering newspaperman, graciously handled some research for me at the Dallas Public Library. He turned up some good 1896 newspaper coverage I did not yet have and took the photograph of William G. Crush's former home in Highland Park that I included in this book.

Melissa Griswold of Amarillo did genealogical research that went a long way toward me being able to flesh out some of the key players in the story, particularly the mysterious Alfred Streeter, the MKT train crew members involved and the victims.

Donaly Brice of Lockhart, retired longtime archivist at the Texas State Library in Austin, looked through months of gubernatorial correspondence and other state records for me.

Lastly, I thank my wonderful partner, Beverly Waak, who contributed a lot to this project, as she has with my other books. Specifically, she helped with research (sometimes finding things I had given up on or hadn't even thought to look for), provided moral and logistical support, gave the first draft its first edit, read the page proofs and did the indexing.

Now, imagine a conductor's loud "All aboard!" and take your seat as a modern-day "excursionist" with a round-trip ticket to learn about one of the more bizarre events in U.S. history, the deliberate crashing together of two speeding steam locomotives in front of forty thousand or more people at a place called Crush.

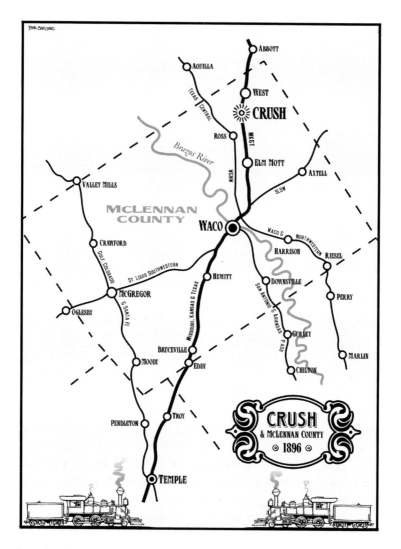

Location of the short-lived town of Crush, Texas, in relation to other communities in McLennan County in 1896, as well as the rail lines that passed through the county at the time. *Map by Ben Sargent.*

THE VIEW FROM THE BARN

Joseph had barely turned nine, but he knew for a certainty that if he obeyed his papa's stern warning he would miss out on something truly amazing.

It just wouldn't be safe, Czech immigrant John Foit declared in forbidding his only son from joining the building crowd. But what impact could the possibility of harm have on an excited Texas farm boy still too young to fully comprehend his mortality? He had watched all the workers getting things ready and heard his parents, neighbors and classmates talk about little else for more than two weeks. Now, on this late summer afternoon, thousands and thousands of men and women milled around on the portion of his father's land that lay along the railroad tracks three miles south of the small McLennan County farming community of West. Looking out a window of their farmhouse, Joseph figured that even the sting of his father's razor strop would be a fair price to pay for witnessing what so many people had come from all over to see.

As soon as his father left the house to join the throng, the boy waited until his mother wasn't looking, eluded his two bossy older sisters and quietly slipped outside. Then he ran as fast as he could straight for their barn. Once inside, he quickly climbed the ladder to the hayloft.

Moving across the creaking, seed- and stem-covered boards, he sat down just far enough inside the open hay door to conceal himself from view. He took in the fantastic scene below. Sweat soaked his overalls, but he didn't care. He had never in his life seen so many people, not even in the county seat at Waco on an always busy Saturday. With a perfect bird's-eye view, the youngster settled in to wait for the show to begin. When it was over, he would slip back to the house and no one would be the wiser.

What he saw that afternoon from his second-story vantage point turned out to be far more than he or anyone else who had come there that day had expected. For the rest of his long life, Joseph Foit would never forget what happened on September 15, 1896.

Only after it was over did he realize that his mother had been standing right behind him the whole time.

KATY COMES TO TEXAS

When young engineer Pat Tobin eased the first tall-stacked steam locomotive across the untested new rail bridge spanning the Red River and the wood-burner panted and puffed south toward the infant town of Denison, it was just another day on the job.

Sixty years later, it was different. Sitting as guest engineer in the cab of the Texas Special as the Missouri-Kansas-Texas Railway's ("MKT" or "Katy") premier passenger train sped toward Denison, the still sharp eighty-year-old realized the true significance of the line's 1872 arrival in Texas and the part he had played in that.

Tobin's ride on Christmas Day 1932 from Durant, Oklahoma, back to his adopted hometown received extensive newspaper coverage. A writer for the *Houston Chronicle* sought to put the MKT's sixty-year anniversary into perspective: "How the then small…railroad finally achieved its goal by forcing its way through an undeveloped country to connect the Northern markets with the gulf, is a story of unusual perseverance, courage and resourcefulness, regarded by many students of the state's early history as an inspiring epic of the Southwest."

For most of 1872, in the form of two parallel iron rails laid across open prairie, the transportation connection that would transform the region moved steadily south through what is now Oklahoma toward Texas. "No time was wasted with ballast and such fripperies," an in-house history of the rail line admitted nearly a century later. "Down went the track on virgin soil whose only packing had been achieved under the hooves of countless cattle

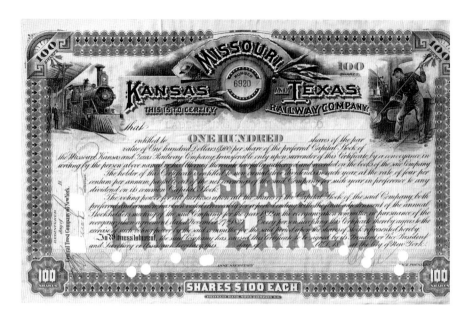

Above: Vintage MKT stock certificate. The railroad was organized in 1870 but did not become a Texas corporation until 1891. *Author's collection.*

Left: "We're Going to Kansas and Texas" declares this early Katy advertisement. The MKT reached Texas in 1872. *Author's collection.*

coming up the Texas trail and by wandering herds of buffalo that quickly became extinct as the railroads despoiled their patrimony."

Despite the economic and social impact the MKT would have, the work on what would be the Lone Star State's first link to the nation's rapidly expanding rail network at first received only minimal notice in the newspapers. "The [rail]road is now completed to Red River, over which it passes on a large iron bridge, and by Dec. 1, will be completed five miles South of this stream to Denison, Texas, which is the point of junction with the Houston & Texas Central Railroad," the *Nashville (TN) Union and American* noted on November 16, 1872, on an inside page.

Track-laying across Indian Territory progressed slower than expected, so it was not until Christmas Eve that a locomotive engineer originally from Vermont named P.H. (Pat) Tobin ran a work train heavily laden with rails and ties to the three-month-old town site named for George Denison, vice-president of the MKT. The Irish American engineer's only task was to deliver supplies to rail workers at the end of the line. The official hoopla would come on Christmas Day, when the first passenger train would be arriving. Still, appreciating that the work train would be the first train to reach Texas, railroad employees and locals who didn't want to miss out on being a part of history packed the southbound train.

An early postcard image of Denison, Texas, the first headquarters of the MKT in the state. *Author's collection.*

Nearing fast-growing Denison—albeit still mostly just a scattering of tents and wooden false-front buildings surrounded by a short thicket of wooden stakes marking newly surveyed lots—the nineteen-year-old at the throttle of the locomotive tied down the train's whistle so folks would know that Denison's first-ever train was on its way to town. Hearing the shrill, steady whistle blast, people rushed to the newly built frame depot to be on hand for the work train's arrival. The train wheezed and clanked to a stop amid a chorus of huzzahs, but there was no ribbon to cut, speeches to listen to or toasts to make. The formalities had been set for Christmas Day, when engine Number 15 would be bringing the first passenger train to town.

As it turned out, bad weather on December 25—it was cold enough to discomfit shaggy buffalo—delayed that official first train. By the time the locomotive finally pulled into the Denison depot with three coaches and a Pullman car carrying about one hundred passengers, it was dark and too late to do anything more than enjoy a community-sponsored holiday feast of freshly killed wild turkey and venison. Still mindful of the occasion, after supper the more exuberant of the visitors repaired to one or another of the several saloons for a round of toasts to the future of Denison, the Lone Star State, one another's health and anything else that came to mind.

"The first through train from the north over the M.K.&T. Railway arrived in our city Christmas night at 7 o'clock," the recently founded *Denison News* ho-hummed the next day.

Organized by New York capitalists in May 1870, with entangling roots going back as far as 1852, the MKT had taken seven years to reach Texas. Another three months after that passed before workers completed nine miles of track linking Denison to Sherman, the northern terminus of the Texas Central Railroad, in March 1873. With that, as the *Chicago Tribune* reported on June 18, 1873, "a continuous line is now in existence from Chicago to Galveston, one thousand two hundred and twenty-eight miles." The MKT owned only a portion of that trackage, but the Illinois city, still recovering from the deadly fire of 1871, now had a rail link to the Gulf of Mexico. Conversely, Texas had a rail connection to the rest of the nation.

Prior to the MKT's coming, Texas could claim only 591 miles of intrastate track. Most of that steel belonged to the Houston & Texas Central Railroad, a line that extended from Galveston on the coast via Houston to Bremond in East Texas, with tracks slowly progressing north toward Sherman. In 1871, the railroad had completed tracks tying Austin to its system as well. But until the MKT arrived, there had been no way for a traveler to reach Texas by rail. The nearest sizable city with rail service was New Orleans, from which a westbound traveler could take a train only as far as Brashear, Louisiana. From there, passengers had to travel by stagecoach to the Morgan Line steamship docks for passage to Galveston.

The MKT transformed Texas and turned Denison into a boomtown. Only one hundred days after its founding, the new railroad town had a population of three thousand and, within five years, twice that. The great cattle drives from South Texas along the multibranched Western and Chisholm Trails that led to railroad connections in Kansas would continue for another half decade or so, but the number of cowboy-pushed longhorns moving north on their four hooves began to decrease with the advent of rail service in Texas. As thousands of head of cattle headed north through Denison to market in slated wooden stock cars, thousands of people coming from the other direction migrated to Texas in somewhat more comfortable frame passenger coaches.

"As soon as the Missouri, Kansas & Texas Ry., crossed the Red River, a stream of immigration, which the most sanguine had not hoped for, set in," *Scribner's Monthly* reported in its July 1873 issue. "The tracts of fertile, black-wax land, which literally needed but to be tickled with the plow to smile a

Postcard image of the MKT's Denison, Texas roundhouse. *Author's collection.*

Bird's Eye View, Denison, Texas.

Bird's-eye view of Denison showing the MKT Depot. *Author's collection.*

harvest, were rapidly taken up, and Denison sprang into existence as the chief town of the newly developed region."

With Denison as its Texas headquarters, the MKT proceeded to expand, either by putting down more track or by negotiating usage agreements with other rail lines. In 1877, five years after the MKT reached Denison, the company began construction of a line to Greenville in Hunt County. From there, after acquiring in the mid-1880s a short line that connected Greenville and Dallas, the MKT had access to that fast-growing city on the Trinity River. A line that would eventually connect Denison with Wichita Falls to the west was begun in 1879. That trackage passed through the town of Whitesboro, where a joint-use contract with the Texas & Pacific Railroad enabled the MKT to connect with Fort Worth, which at that time was the nation's largest cattle center.

In 1880, eight years after the MKT reached Texas, financier Jay Gould's Missouri Pacific Railroad leased the MKT and the company lost virtually all its identity. The absorbed line was operated by MoPAC as its Kansas-Texas division, or the K-T. Soon, it occurred to someone how much "K-T" sounded like Katy, and the railroad acquired the feminine nickname that would last for as long as the railroad itself did. Meanwhile, the line continued to expand. In 1881, though a track-use agreement with the Gould-controlled

International and Great Northern Railroad, Katy passenger trains steamed into the busy depot at San Antonio for the first time. Also in 1881, the Katy began building track from Fort Worth via Hillsboro to Waco. At the same time, the company was extending a line south from Dallas, also destined for Waco. That city lay on the Brazos River in the heart of the state's cotton-producing country and was becoming a major railroad crossroad.

A portion of the Hillsboro-to-Waco route surveyed by the railroad happened to cut through the 260 acres of rich farmland owned by one Thomas Marion West, a Kentuckian who had settled in northeastern McLennan County in 1859. Like others interested in growing and selling crops, particularly cotton, wheat and maize, what attracted him to the area was a robust water source known as Bold Springs. ("Bold" being a corruption of the last name of another early settler, Carey Boulds.) A community soon developed nearby, taking Bold Springs as its name. With a population of three, by 1860 it had a store, a blacksmith shop, churches and a post office with West as postmaster. When the Civil War broke out, West volunteered for service in the Confederate army and rose to the rank of captain. After the war, he returned to his land and soon married a woman who had lost her first husband during the conflict.

With the approach of the railroad, West sold the MKT some of his land for a depot and subdivided additional acreage along the recently laid tracks for development as a townsite. The community of Bold Springs dried up, and the new town came to be called West. Thanks to the just-arrived MKT, West the man and West the town both prospered. The town's namesake opened the first general store and later owned a bank, a furniture store and a hotel.

In addition to stimulating business activity in general, the Katy gave Central Texas farmers and ranchers a more efficient way of getting their commodities to market. Also, and of lasting significance on the culture of the town of West, the line brought in a substantial number of Czechs and German immigrants eager to acquire good farmland. For a village with such an American-sounding name as West, the community soon had a decidedly European feel, with caraway seed–flavored klobasa (sausage) and sweet fruit-filled kolaches more common than bacon and biscuits at the breakfast table.

Traffic through the community of West increased as the railroad moved on from Waco via Temple, Granger, Taylor, Bastrop, Smithville and LaGrange in the general direction of Houston. Meanwhile, a series of court cases forced Gould to divest himself of the MKT in 1888. No longer part of the Missouri Pacific, the MKT went into voluntary receivership before reorganizing as a Texas corporation known as the Missouri, Kansas & Texas Railway on July 1, 1891.

Prior to its incorporation in Texas, the MKT's receivers approved a new company logo, a design submitted by the Rand McNally Company of Chicago. In the emblem, "THE M.K. AND T." appeared in bold white letters over a red herald. Running at an angle beneath the initials was a ribbon bearing the company's full name. Beneath that lay a palm frond, possibly intended to be symbolic of the company's intent to connect the Midwest and Texas with the Gulf of Mexico. While the MKT logo (with some later streamlining) would stand as the company's brand identifier for the rest of its corporate life, what the public would remember most was the Katy girl. In most of its early advertising, the company began using a drawing featuring an attractive young woman in the traveling clothes of the era. Clearly, she was Katy.

By the late summer of 1893, the Katy was placing long, one-column ads in the state's larger newspapers touting the line's reach as well as the modernity and comfort of its rolling stock. "Many Texans are not aware of the fact that [the MKT] was the first railroad to cross the border of Texas (from any direction) and push into the interior and on to the deep water on the Mexican Gulf; but such was the case," the ad pointed out. It was also a fact, the ad continued, that "the KATY is the first to get out of the old ruts and improve its facilities for handling passengers and freight."

This ad for the MKT's premier passenger train, the Katy Flyer, features the company's iconic Katy girl. Her wardrobe would change, but she lasted just about as long as the railroad did. *Author's collection.*

Less than a year later, in the spring of 1894, the Katy had connected with surging St. Louis, which soon would jump from the fifth- to the fourth-largest city in the United States with a population of more than 575,000. Having trackage to Kansas City as well, the Katy now extended all the way south to Houston on its own rails and from the Bayou City to Galveston via access rights negotiated with the Galveston, Houston & Henderson Railroad after the MKT obtained 49 percent ownership of that line. With 2,650 Texas-based employees, the Katy now operated on 2,147 miles of track in three states and one territory, having grown into a major regional carrier.

Even though the Katy mainline passed through the little town of West, it was just a dot on the railway's system map seemingly consigned to obscurity by its name. When people heard "West, Texas," they tended to overlook the comma, instead picturing the western half of the very large state the community stood near the center of. But fifteen years after its founding, thanks to the Katy, West would acquire a lasting claim to fame by being the closest town to the scene of one of the more unusual incidents in Texas history. Thomas West, who would live until 1912, was probably there to see it.

THE NOT-SO-GAY NINETIES

A quarter century passed before the last decade of the nineteenth century began to be referred to as the "Gay Nineties."

Only sixteen on the final day of 1899, Illinois-born Richard Culter went on to become a nationally known artist. By the time he turned nineteen, having studied art domestically and in France, he had his own studio in New York and soon ranked as one of the premier magazine illustrators of the day. In 1925, commissioned by *LIFE* magazine to do a series of drawings of scenes and people representative of the 1890s, Culter is generally credited with coining the phrase that came to be the prime descriptor of the 1890s. Two years after the *LIFE* series began, he put the term on library shelves across the country with the publication of his book, *The Gay Nineties: An Album of Reminiscent Drawings*.

While Culter may have viewed his early teenage years with a natural-enough nostalgia, using the word *Gay* (in its original meaning of "carefree") to characterize the 1890s is about as accurate as labeling the World War II era the "Fun Forties." In truth, it would be hard to come up with a single phrase truly capturing the 1890s. Viewing those ten years through lenses free of roseate tint, the Gay Nineties could much more accurately be characterized as a period of cultural and technological transition overlaid by dire financial times and polarizing political issues. In the United States, the decade saw the fading of the western frontier and the end of the Indian wars; rapidly advancing technology (aspirin, X-rays, wireless telegraphy, "horseless carriages" and more); a period of terrible economic hardship for millions of

Americans; violent labor unrest and crippling railroad strikes; a particularly heated presidential election in 1896; and an assortment of zany events that still stand as some of the more bizarre in American history. Finally, the decade ended with the nation's first overseas conflict—the Spanish-American War— and its emergence as a world power. In short, most Americans who lived through the decade as adults could hardly call the 1890s gay. Not that the decade didn't have its complement of the glitzy and gaudy.

Approved by Congress in 1890, following a period of stiff competition between Chicago and New York, the much-publicized World's Columbia Exposition would have a huge cultural impact on the nation. Covering 633 acres along the city's Lake Michigan front and dominated by a 233-foot-tall Ferris wheel—the world's first—the event attracted 27 million visitors. They came from all over the United States and the world to take in an event intended to showcase the nation's progress four hundred years after the arrival of Columbus in the New World.

Popularly known as the White City because of its white stucco buildings and extensive electrical lighting, the fair would be a tribute to the latest in technology as well as the culture of the day. But event planners did not hesitate in offering more low-brow entertainment. Inspired by the 1889 Paris Universal Exposition, the fair featured a mile-and-a-half-long, block-wide corridor called the "Midway Plaisance." It would demonstrate the progress of man by exhibiting what were viewed as more primitive cultures. Visitors could see Bedouin villages, Egyptian dancers (including the famed Little Egypt), South Sea islanders, Asians, Laplanders, "The World's Congress of Beauties…40 Women from 40 Nations," African tribesmen and much more. Fair organizers also licensed vendors to cater to the masses with everything from food and drink to souvenir stands. Not officially part of the fair but located just outside its grounds, even more sleazy carnival booths drew large crowds. Also not part of the fair, the Buffalo Bill's Wild West Show did a flourishing business adjacent to the exposition site.

By the time the fair closed and Buffalo Bill left town, the nation's economy was on the verge of a financial depression not exceeded in severity until the Great Depression following the stock market collapse of 1929. One of the factors in the economic downturn of the early 1890s was an illness afflicting the industry that had fueled a period of unparalleled growth while uniting the nation, at least in a transportation sense, following the Civil War: the railroads. With some 190,000 miles of rail line, including three transcontinental routes—the Union Pacific, the Northern Pacific and the Southern Pacific—the railroad industry had been the dominant factor in

The 1893 Chicago World's Fair and its Midway Plaisance catered to both high and low tastes. *Chicago Public Library*.

the nation's explosive industrial growth in the 1880s. The word *bubble* as a descriptor for an inflated segment of the economy doomed to pop sooner or later had not yet entered the vernacular, but overbuilding and shaky financing led to a series of railroad bankruptcies and bank failures in 1893 that had a domino effect on the economy.

In addition to the Southern Pacific, which entered Texas east of Beaumont and continued for more than eight hundred miles through Houston, San Antonio and El Paso, the Lone Star State had nearly nine thousand miles of track owned or leased by thirty-six railroad lines, from short lines to major interstate carriers. Most of the state's more than 2 million residents lived in rural areas, but thanks to the network of iron rails, many of its cities were experiencing fast growth. The biggest was Dallas, with a population of 38,067, closely followed by San Antonio with 37,653 residents. Galveston ranked as the third-largest city with 29,084 people, edging out Houston at 27,557 residents. Rounding out the top five was Fort Worth, with 23,076 people calling it home.

The difficulty the railroad companies had in the first half of the 1890s is reflected in the miles of track built in Texas at the time. While mileage nearly tripled from 1880 to 1890 (3,025 to 8,667) from 1890 to 1900 all the lines operating in the state added only 1,171 miles of track.

Railroad expansion had transformed Texas, but by the early 1890s, many people had come to realize that the railroad industry was not necessarily some loving, altruistic enterprise engineered solely to bring growth and prosperity. The "roads," as they were often referred to before paved highways, were about making money for their stockholders. Many Americans, wary of anything more powerful than the people, began to see railroads as soulless corporate entities that charged more than they should because they could, fixed routes and rates, sold stock for far more than it was worth and, to make all that easier, had many national, state and local politicians in their proverbial cash-heavy canvas mail pouches.

As the public began to resent the very oil- and soot-smeared hand that fed it, a movement arose in Texas to regulate the railroad. Whether to do that or not became a major issue of the state's 1890 gubernatorial election. Not only did voters approve a constitutional amendment mandating such an agency, they elected a former newspaper editor turned lawyer named James S. Hogg to make it happen.

The legislature passed the enabling measure in 1891, creating the nation's first state level railroad regulatory agency, the Texas Railroad Commission. The new law gave the commission regulatory authority over railroad rates and operations of railroads and express companies, as well as terminals and wharves. The statutory agency would have three commissioners. When Hogg asked U.S. Senator John H. Reagan if he would be interested in chairing the commission, he accepted and resigned his senatorial seat to take on the job.

Though hampered by bare-bones funding, several adverse court decisions and the fact that it had only intrastate authority, the new commission did succeed in holding down intrastate freight rates. Despite its name, however, the commission had no power to regulate other matters involving the industry, including railroad safety.

Naturally enough, not everyone supported state railroad regulation (especially the railroads, those with railroad jobs or elected officials supported by railroads), so Hogg had to fight to stay in office when the 1892 election approached. His opponent, Waco-based attorney George W. Clark, was supported by the railroads, several of which he represented, including the MKT.

In 1892, Austin attorney William M. Walton traveled to Giddings to address the people of Lee County in a courthouse speech. Walton did not seek office, but he supported Clark for governor. Walton also favored a major tweaking of the railroad commission's enabling legislature, the impact of which would dilute the commission's power. The extent of its regulation aside, in an eloquent sentence quoted in the *Galveston News* on May 11, 1892, the lawyer nicely summarized the impact the railroads had on Texas: "They are the arms of capital and reach out together…[to] quicken the pulse of commerce, drive the frontiers back, aid the producer and cheapen all things to the consumer… they bring prosperity as much so as the plans of the carpenter and the sledge-hammer of the blacksmith."

Hogg won the bitter election, and the railroad commission survived. In 1894, the same year the U.S. Supreme Court upheld the state's authority to create such an entity, the legislature made railroad commissioner an elective office with members serving staggered six-year terms. Already answerable to the federal Interstate Commerce Commission, railroads did not like an added layer of regulation in Texas. But they had other, broader problems.

While most railroads tried to adhere to their schedules as strictly as possible, that did not necessarily mean every line enjoyed overall good management. Engineers worked to see that track laying proceeded as efficiently as possible between points A and B and Z, but many of the corporations they worked for were a can of twisting worms—or snakes. Building virtual monopolies through lease agreements, New York financiers like Jay Gould ruthlessly ran their transportation empires, competing for freight and passenger business.

Soon, business growth slowed to a near standstill, the nation's economy sinking faster than the boiler water level in a high-balling steam locomotive. The depression of 1894, which began with a stock market crash in May 1893 that came to be called the Panic of 1893, hit Americans much harder than the financial downturn twenty years before (the Panic of 1873). Hundreds of banks failed, and thousands of businesses went belly up. Of the nation's 364 railroads, 89 went bankrupt. In 1894, unemployment in the United States exceeded 18 percent.

The January 1, 1894 edition of the *Galveston News* carried a story headlined, "The Nation's Unemployed." Rewritten from the *St. Louis Republic*, it quoted Chauncey M. Depew, president of Cornelius Vanderbilt's New York Central Railroad, on the state of the economy. "I have been through all the panics of the last 30 years," he pronounced, "but I have never seen one in which the distress was so widespread and reached so many people who previously had not been affected as this panic of 1893."

The attorney went on to say that more than 2 million Americans were without jobs. Calculating five persons per family, he added, "[T]hat means 10 million people with no bread winner among them." The article continued: "From statements printed in other papers in other cities aside from New York, it is not believed Mr. Depew has overstated the wide spread desolation which overshadows the hearts and homes of so many of our fellow citizens."

The beginning of a new year is traditionally a time of reflection, positive resolution and optimistic good cheer. But in the normally busy port city of Galveston, hundreds of homeless, hungry people crowded the streets and alleys. They had no jobs and little prospect of one.

On New Year's Eve, a local real estate broker, a man of some means, was out for a stroll with a lady friend when a man approached and asked if they could talk. Seeing that the man was destitute, the broker told him he would return to help him as soon as he walked his companion home. When he came back as promised, the homeless man was gone. Moved by the fellow's plight, on New Year's Day the broker went to the police station and gave the chief one hundred meal tickets he had purchased at a local restaurant and told him to give them to people who needed them.

A *Galveston News* reporter interviewed the chief, who said that the homeless people he encountered were not traditional tramps. They were mostly out-of-work tradesmen or dock workers who tried hard to maintain their dignity and did not resort to crime or aggressive begging. A few days earlier, the chief had gone to the scene of an attempted suicide near the port's large grain elevator. An unemployed man had slashed his wrists and jumped from a moving railroad box car but survived. "I asked him why he wanted to kill himself," the chief said. "He said that he was out of work and could get none. For several days he had lived on cottonseed hulls and raw wheat that he had picked up in box cars."

On January 19, the Galveston City Council voted to sell $15,000 in bonds, with the proceeds going to "grading and filling [city streets] to provide work for destitute citizens." One alderman said at least 1,500 "bona fide citizens of this city are out of work and suffering for the necessities of life."

Even when the economy finally—if slowly—began turning around, the nation's monetary policy was the primary point of contention in American politics and the overarching issue of the 1896 presidential campaign that pitted William McKinley of Ohio against the "great commoner" from Nebraska, William Jennings Bryan.

This political cartoon nicely captures the financial crisis of the first half of the 1890s. The big debate centered on gold versus silver as the nation's currency base, but that was academic for millions of out-of-work Americans. *Author's collection.*

The debate revolved around the complex issue of gold versus silver as the basis for the nation's currency, and it was as polarizing as anything the nation had seen since the Civil War. During that conflict, the federal government had for the first time begun issuing paper money backed only by the credibility of the U.S. government as opposed to gold and silver. That helped fund the war effort by increasing the money supply, but it also created inflation. After the war, the nation returned to a combination of gold and silver coinage, but in 1873, Congress passed an act demonetizing silver. The unintended consequence of a gold-only standard was a severe economic downturn, as the money supply became extremely tight. That led to an 1877 law reviving silver coinage on a 16:1 value ratio with gold, a system known as bimetallism. A flood of newly mined silver increased the money supply, along with inflation. To cure that, in 1890 Congress passed the Sherman Silver Purchase Act, which required the government to buy millions of ounces of silver for conversion to coinage. That buying was done with gold notes. Gold being far more valuable than silver, the result was a run on the nation's treasury that came perilously close to emptying it. The Panic of 1893 followed, with mega-rich J.P. Morgan bailing out the government to avoid its default. In the run-up to the 1896 election, the conservative business community (which supported McKinley) wanted a return to a strictly gold-based currency. Farmers and others of the working class (who supported Bryan) favored bimetallism. The battle raged until McKinley got elected president and the nation returned to the gold standard.

Whatever the basis of the nation's currency, by the mid-1890s the divide between the "haves" and the "have nots" had never been wider. But a person's economic standing did not seem to have an impact on their appetite for entertainment. If anything, the dismal years of 1893–95 (actually, from 1873 to 1896 the economy was in recession 50 percent of the time) had practically made escapism a national pastime. Circuses and scores of Wild West shows flourished, as did prizefighting, baseball and the relatively new collegiate sport of football.

Buffalo Bill's Wild West Show drew big crowds across the nation, but not all the gunplay involved shooting blanks. In August 1895, the notorious outlaw John Wesley Hardin met a violent demise in an El Paso saloon. One of the Old West's most vicious killers, credited with gunning down a few dozen men give or take, Hardin had been released from state prison in 1894 after serving fourteen years for killing a sheriff's deputy in 1874. Behind bars he had read the law, and soon after entering the free world again, he passed the state bar exam. He didn't shoot anyone else after leaving prison, but Hardin continued his old habits of drinking and gambling until El Paso constable John Selman—extending payback over a grudge—shot him to death while standing at a bar shooting craps.

Less than a year after Hardin's death made headlines, El Paso gained more national attention when Governor Charles Culberson used the legendary Texas Rangers to prevent another kind of fight from happening in his state. Early in 1896, a Dallas promoter named Dan Stuart began trying to put together a championship match between world champion Robert Fitzsimmons and challenger Peter Maher. Prizefighting having been made illegal in Texas the previous fall, Stuart decided to stage his "Fistic Carnival" in Juarez, Mexico, across the border from El Paso.

But the governor of the Mexican state of Chihuahua backed off his initial promise to allow the fight, and Congress hastily passed a law making prizefights illegal in New Mexico and other U.S. territories. Having no hope of pulling off the match in the United States or Mexico, Stuart hit on the idea of staging the bout on an island in the middle of the Rio Grande—an international no-man's land exempt from the law.

After consulting with the crusty Roy Bean, the justice of the peace at a lively rail stop in Val Verde County called Langtry, Stuart arranged for the fight to be held on an international sandbar within rifle range of Bean's combination saloon, store and office. Shortly before midnight on February 20, an eastbound train with two engines and twenty fully loaded passenger coaches left the El Paso station for the secret fight location. On board were Stuart and his staff, the fighters and their trainers, the press, the Rangers and sports still willing to pay twenty dollars for a ticket and another twelve for the train ride.

After the train reached Langtry, about two-thirds of the distance between El Paso and San Antonio, the Rangers could only watch from Texas soil as the much-ballyhooed fight finally took place on the island. While the fight, which Fitzsimmons won by knocking Maher out in the first round, disappointed all observers, it did prove that there was always a ready audience willing to pay to see something novel.

Boxing had been around for centuries, but in Chicago, more than 1,500 miles from the semi-desert of West, Texas, someone was pondering a new and bizarre form of crowd-pleasing combat. What he envisioned would in comparison make a bare-knuckled prizefight look like a *pas de deux*, a duel ballet.

WORKIN' ON THE RAILROAD

William Cowper Brann, outspoken publisher of a vitriol-drenched monthly he called *Brann's Iconoclast*, never lacked for an opinion.

In 1894, an itinerant journalist originally from Illinois, Brann had moved to fast-growing Waco as chief editorial writer for that city's *Daily News*. The following year, he left his day job to revive the *Iconoclast*, which he had published for a time a few years earlier in Austin. In what he called his "journal of personal protest," he feuded in print with the president of Baylor College, a Baptist school, and railed against all that he did not believe in. Though a rabid supporter of the Jim Crow status quo who had nothing kind to say about African Americans, not to mention Episcopalians or the British, Brann was an intelligent, well-read man who knew how to turn a phrase. The name of his publication could not have been a better description of his personality. Nor was his iconoclastic nature anything new.

When he was only ten, as Brann later confessed in one of his essays, "I was so infatuated with locomotives that to get possession of one I stole an entire freight train." As he recalled, the train's crew had abandoned the train "to investigate a big watermelon that the station agent had opened."

With the railroad men thus occupied, sweet juice dripping down their chins, Brann climbed into the steam engine's cab and looked wide-eyed at the array of gauges, valves, levers and all the other indicators or controls necessary for the operation of the locomotive. "I had no intention of meddling with the iron monster but when I got my hand on the lever the temptation to set the big drivers in motion was too strong to be resisted," he wrote.

A diamond stack steam locomotive similar to the engines used by the MKT from the 1870s until the last decade of the nineteenth century. *Author's collection.*

The train moved away from the station so gently that the watermelon-eating crew did not notice. Deciding, as he recalled, that he had "rather be hanged as an old sheep than a lamb," he pulled back on the throttle to increase steam and immediately felt the train pick up speed. To add to the moment, he rang the bell and joyfully blew the whistle. "Delirious with joy," he was hanging out the right window of the cab, sitting in the engineer's seat, when suddenly and forcefully someone pulled him in by his ear.

Fortunately for that railroad line, the conductor had opted for a nap in the caboose rather than watermelon and had stayed behind. When he woke up to the realization that his train was not only moving but picking up speed, he walked along the tops of the rocking box cars until he reached the cab. There, as Brann put it, he intended to vigorously "expostulate" with the engineer for pulling out of the station without comparing train orders—a serious breach of company rules. Then he discovered that young Brann had hijacked his train and quickly brought the boy's joy ride to a halt.

Brann wrote that the events that transpired after he was returned to his parents "could not possibly possess the absorbing interest for the general public that they did for me." Then he moved on to the main point of his essay, which was to canonize the working men who ran the trains. "The locomotive engineer is to the village-bred boy of today what the stage-driver was to the youth of his grandsire," Brann wrote. "The brakeman who can

Engineers and conductors were the ranking men on any train. Inelegantly known by their fellow railroad men as "hoggers," engineers were folk heroes in the age of steam. *Author's collection.*

ride all day on top of a box car, and the passenger-train conductor with his gaudy cap and Mardi Gras lantern, pale into insignificance beside the man who manages the iron horse."

Though critical of so much when it came to American politics, certain institutions and society, Brann clearly had no issues with trainmen, especially the men who sat at the throttle. "The…engineers constitute a peculiar class that is neither understood nor appreciated by the general public," Brann wrote. "Sober, silent, alert, with the time-table for their Bible and the train dispatcher's written orders for their creed, they discharge their dangerous duty."

Dangerous was the operative word for all railroad workers, not just engineers. In 1895, the fatality rate for American trainmen was 6.45 per 1,000. Two years earlier, when Congress passed the first national railroad safety legislation, 1,567 railroad workers died on the job nationwide, with

Working as a fireman was a hard and dangerous job, but the promotional ladder usually led to the engineer's seat. This engraving of a Katy fireman was printed on an early MKT stock certificate. *Author's collection.*

another 18,877 injured. In Texas alone, between June 30, 1896, and June 30, 1897, 56 railroad employees lost their lives on duty (9 of those men worked for the Katy). Despite the risk, "There was a fascination about railroading that hard work and low pay could not dim," Edgar A. Custer wrote in his autobiography, *No Royal Road*.

Steam locomotives were only large, powerful machines, but engineers tended to see them as living things they had been entrusted to care for. "She had a soul," an old engineer reflected, "and there was a bond between her and the engineer. In the cab on a moonlit night, seeing the light flashing on the rods, the flames dancing in the firebox, looking back at the smoke trailing over the train, the steam gauge at 200 pounds, and hearing that old girl talking in the language only she and you understood—there was nothing like it in the world."

Whether running a ballast-scorching freight train or—flagged for a direct run—pulling his line's fastest and most luxurious passenger coaches, an engineer (known in railroad slang as a "hogger") understood that all manner of bad things could happen on his watch. His train could plow into an animal, person or conveyance trying to cross the tracks in front of him; his train could derail due to human error or mechanical fault; or his train could collide head-on with another fast train. All of those eventualities usually meant death or injury, particularly in the case of two locomotives smashing into each other cowcatcher-to-cowcatcher. Beyond collisions, railroad men died when they fell off trains, got crushed between cars or were fatally injured in any number of other ways.

Preventing head-on collisions was largely a matter of strict adherence to schedule and the diligence of train dispatchers. But guarding against a boiler explosion—by far the most catastrophic thing that could happen to a steam locomotive—was the cabin crew's job. There were multiple devices and appliances on the engine intended to avoid an explosion, but the main line of defense was always the constant and careful attention of the engine crew to the water level in the boiler. An average-size locomotive's boiler was a cylinder containing a few thousand gallons of water, through which multiple steel tubes passed hot gases from the firebox in back to the smokebox in front, heating the water to make the steam. That steam, at a pressure of (typically) 200 psi, powered the locomotive. The firebox, heated to about two thousand degrees Fahrenheit, was insulated on the front, back, top and sides, with spaces containing water. If the water in the boiler dropped to a point where the hot firebox was exposed and no longer insulated, the metal burned through quickly, and the water in the boiler turned to steam all at once. Since water turning into steam expands its volume by a factor of 1,600, the effect was instantaneous and violently explosive. It usually propelled the boiler right off the frame, taking with it everything between the smokebox and tender—including, unfortunately, the crew.

While the engineer answered to the train conductor, it was the man in the denim overalls and thin-striped soft cap who made the train go. Sitting on the right side of a locomotive, the engineer controlled the throttle, reversing gear, the brakes and the steam whistle. From monitoring boiler pressure (along with the fireman) to overseeing lubrication and other aspects of maintenance, he was responsible for just about everything that involved running the train.

Writer-historian Marquis James (he won a 1929 Pulitzer Prize for his biography of Texas hero Sam Houston) grew up in the steam engine era. Late in his career, James recalled a train trip from Oklahoma to Texas via a branch of the Chicago, Rock Island & Pacific Railroad. During that ride, he remembered that "the porters, waiters, news butcher, and conductor all spoke about the engineer's awesome reputation as a 'fast roller.'"

On this occasion, James explained, the train was running late, but the man the train crew referred to as Ol' Gilroy "whooped along, scorching the banks of the Canadian River, twenty minutes between stations that were scheduled half an hour apart. The passengers, initially worried that they would not reach Fort Worth on time, began to relax."

But suddenly the train slowed perceptibly. "They put the orders on him," one of the porters said ruefully. That meant that the conductor had walked through the swaying cars to the locomotive to remind the engineer of the written instructions on train movements issued by the dispatcher. When a train stopped, how long it waited and how slow or fast it went were not up to the engineer except in the advent of an emergency. The man at the throttle had to follow train orders if he wanted to remain employed.

Hearing so much about Ol' Gilroy made James curious to see the "hogger" before he got off the train. James made his way to the front of the train so he could take a look at the man occupying the right-hand seat in the cab. It turned out that Gilroy was not old at all. To the contrary, he was surprisingly young. Still, James thought he looked like an engineer should. Wearing a long-billed railroad cap and a red bandanna around his neck, the engineer walked with a swagger born of confidence and experience, not posturing.

"And there you have a clear…snapshot of the steam engineer," James wrote years later. "Self-confident, adventurous, and debonair—a hot pilot, speed racer, and T-formation quarterback, all in one.…Was it any surprise that young boys saw him as a sort of deity?" Without doubt, the writer continued, the engineer was "obviously the most important and interesting man on the railroad."

The second of the three occupants of any locomotive cab was the fireman, often called a "tallow pot" because he used a long-nosed container full of liquid tallow (later oil) to lubricate the engine's numerous valves. Railroad firemen did not put out fires—their primary job was to keep them going. They sat on the left side of the engine, monitoring steam pressure, the level of water in the boiler and, in the early days, shoveling coal as necessary. "Handling black diamonds" was a common railroader's euphemism for the job. In addition, the fireman was supposed to watch for signals and any obstructions on the track ahead.

"In some respects, the fireman is the most important man on a train," Herbert Hamblem wrote of railroading in the 1890s in his memoir, *The General Manager's Story*. "Not only do all engineers invariably depend on him to perform many of the duties properly belonging to themselves, but he it is who bends his back and hustles to make steam to get the train in on time."

Working as a fireman was a hot, hard job. "For pure drudgery, low pay, chronic danger, and debased social standing," Richard Reinhardt wrote in *Workin' on the Railroad: Reminiscences from the Age of Steam*, "the job of firing a steam locomotive was hard to beat." The position did have one saving grace, however. Almost all engineers started out as firemen, the transition period from stoking fireboxes to becoming the "Captain of the Train" a minimum of four years.

Steam trains also would have two brakemen—a head brakeman who sat in the cab behind the fireman and a rear brakeman who stayed in the caboose. Often that brakeman sat in the caboose's cupola so he could see the track ahead and keep an eye out for "hot boxes" indicated by smoke emanating from a hot axle bearing. The rear brakeman also monitored air pressure in the train's brake system. Before air brakes, brakemen had to turn wheels atop the cars to stop a train, a highly dangerous job. Since brakemen also oversaw the coupling of cars, the sad truism was that it was easy to spot a longtime brakeman by looking at his hands. If he had one or two fingers missing, he had spent time coupling and stopping trains.

Train crews and other blue-collar workmen made the trains run, but railroads had to have a managerial structure as well. The hierarchy began with a president, who answered to a corporate board of directors. Next were one or more vice-presidents. At the third level down, a general manager supervised managers who had individual responsibility for the basic components of any line: a superintendent of roadway or chief engineer, who oversaw maintenance of track, bridges and structures; a superintendent of machinery with responsibility for maintenance and operation of all the rolling stock; a superintendent of transportation who handled scheduling and all movement of trains; a car accountant who kept track of the location and movement of cars; a traffic manager who oversaw freight and passenger rates, advertising and business promotion; a comptroller who did the bookkeeping; and the paymaster. In the 1890s, the nation had some 800,000 railroad employees, from general managers to the greenest trainman. The hours were long—twelve hours a day, six days a week—and much of the work was quite dangerous in the days before governmental oversight of railroad safety, but the railroads offered generally steady employment. If a man was willing to work hard and honestly, he usually had a lifetime job if he wanted it. Naturally, layoffs came with economic downturns, but a railroader with a good reputation usually got his job back when conditions improved.

"Railroad men," Reinhardt continued in his book, "are conservative and fraternal. Their community life is introverted, closely woven, and deep-dyed with tradition. To an old-fashioned railroader, honor consists in starting young and working one's way up the ladder. In the age of steam, it was axiomatic that the best locomotive engineers previously had been firemen, the best conductors had risen from brakemen, and the best executives had started at the bottom as callboys, telegraphers, switchmen, or section hands."

More than twenty major trunk lines and scores of short lines ran their trains on roughly 190,000 miles of track, forming an iron web that held the nation together. If a manufacturer needed to send a large order of goods, the load went by rail. If someone needed to travel from one town to another, they either rode a horse, bounced along in a horse- or mule-drawn wagon or buggy or they took a passenger train. Most mail went by rail, as did newspapers and money shipments.

The laying of new tracks could turn open prairie into a boomtown, just as being missed by a railroad could wither a townsite like rain-starved gamma grass. A mid-1890s Denison, Texas city directory contained a bottom-of-the-page house ad, "The Most Important Necessities for a City," that illustrates the point. Beneath that heading, the ad listed eight must-haves for any community: "Good Railways/Plenty of Pure Water/Cheap Fuel/Economical Light Facilities/A Good Hotel/A First Class Newspaper/Good Banks/An Up-to-Date City Directory." While the need for a city directory could be debated, it is no surprise that the first necessity on the list was "Good Railways." For anyone with a stake in a community, whether as a businessperson or simply as a resident interested in employment opportunities and decent amenities, a good railway was any railway at all that came to your town.

"The world was born again with the building of the first locomotive and the laying of the first level iron roadway," E.P. Alexander wrote in *The American Railway*, an overview of the still-growing industry published in 1889. He continued:

> *The energies and activities, the powers and possibilities then developed have acted and reacted in every sphere of life—social, industrial, and political—until human progress, after smoldering like a spark for a thousand years, has burst into a conflagration which will soon leave small trace of the life and customs, or even the modest of thought, which our fathers knew. By bringing men more and more closely together, and supplying them more and more abundantly and cheaply with all the varied treasures of the earth…it adds continually more fuel to the flame it originated.*

Reinhardt amplified that in the introduction to his anthology: "It [the railroad industry] was the great speculator, the political tyrant, the recruiter of immigrants, the opener of new lands, the cynosure of poets and pioneers, the symbol of adventure, opportunity, escape, and power. Not even the government was more ubiquitous, more tangible, and more influential than the railroad."

For many in the 1890s, trains meant more than fast transportation or economic growth. "Many a youth…felt his ambition and imagination stimulated tremendously by the passing of a train through his father's farm," Dallas banker William A. Philpott observed in his book *Cinder in Your Eye and a Hodgepodge Miscellany, Including Jingle Fillers*. "All work would stop (plowing, hoeing, cotton picking) until the passenger train became a speck in the distance or disappeared around a hill. It was a definite connection between the limited horizon and daily tasks of the farm boy and the great outside world, far away places, opportunities to succeed."

Railroads were all that, but what they were really about was generating big money for their owners. A man could make a decent living working for a railroad, but if he wanted to get rich, he wouldn't do it walking through passenger coaches punching tickets. In Chicago, an individual who had worked his way up from brakeman to conductor before becoming a traveling salesman for a railroad equipment company had come up with a crazy idea that just might be his ticket to wealth. It did involve the use of railroad rolling stock, but not in a way anyone had ever thought of before.

RAILROAD WRECK MADE TO ORDER

L ike most current or former railroad men, thirty-four-year-old Alfred L. Streeter had seen his share of train wrecks—either derailments, which railroaders sarcastically referred to as going "in the ditch," or head-end crashes they called "cornfield meets." Derailments were the most common form of railroad accident, followed by collisions.

Other than the financial loss associated with destroyed or damaged rolling stock and cargo, if an accident resulted in no injuries the only consequence was a delay in service until the tracks could be cleared. But when locomotives crashed headlamp-to-headlamp at high speed, train crew members and often passengers died. A significant passenger train accident with fatalities received as much newspaper coverage as disastrous commercial airliner crashes would in future generations. Gawkers rushed to accident scenes to see the predictably spectacular results of mass and velocity gone awry. Often they collected pieces of wreckage as souvenirs. Those who couldn't go to the scene read eagerly about train wrecks in their newspapers or magazines.

Born around 1861 in Wilkes-Barre, Pennsylvania, to William and May Streeter, Alfred Streeter came to Chicago in 1881. Most of his early story and even later life is a mystery, but from his late twenties onward, his story would get increasingly more interesting and he would become much better known—though not in a good way.

Like so many other young men in the closing decades of the nineteenth century, after reaching Illinois, Streeter went to work for the railroad. Its rail connections had made Chicago the teeming metropolis that it was, and quite literally, Chicago was helping to build the railroads. Not only was the city of nearly 1 million home to thousands of railroad workers, by the end of the nineteenth century it had also evolved into one of the nation's primary rail car, parts and equipment manufacturing centers. The largest manufacturer was the Pullman Company, which built both passenger and freight cars. Other plants produced train wheels, brake parts and other rail car components. In addition, railroad supply houses furnished the industry everything from signal lanterns to switches. Those railroad-related industries employed some twelve thousand people in 1890. Another fifteen thousand or so worked directly for the various lines serving the city.

Streeter began his long connection with the railroad industry as a youthful news butch, peddling newspapers, candy, salted peanuts (the better to improve bottled drink sales on his next pass down the aisle), cigars and other items aboard passenger trains. He learned capitalism from the ground up, for instance quickly grasping that newspapers left by departing passengers could be collected and resold. Now a street-smart young man, by 1882 he was working as a brakeman for the Chicago, Milwaukee & St. Paul Railroad. Later, he bossed a railroad wrecking crew, the men whose job it was to clear a train wreck from the tracks using a rolling steam crane they called "the big hook." Eventually—and apparently with all ten of his digits still intact—he worked his way up to passenger train conductor.

By the mid-1890s, Streeter had left his railroad job for a position as a traveling salesman for a Chicago-based railroad equipment company and may have lived for a time in Cleveland, Canton and Columbus, Ohio. In the tough economy of the mid-1890s, most men would have been happy to hold a steady railroad-related job. But Streeter aspired to upward mobility.

While taking in the sights at the 1893 Chicago World's Fair and Buffalo Bill's Wild West Show, he observed that people would pay good money to witness a spectacle of some sort. Be it freaks or cowboys and Indians or a prizefight, it occurred to Streeter that the entertainment world's basic business model was as flexible as Indian rubber. It would work no matter the type of attraction offered, just so long as it was compelling and well hyped. Instead of selling tickets to folks interested in seeing Siamese twins or watching two mustachioed, bare-chested pugilists duke it out amid flying sweat and blood, why not make money by pitting two iron monsters against each other in a duel between fast-moving steam locomotives?

A staged train crash, Streeter believed, could convert twisted iron into money. Who cared if it was a gold or silver-based currency? All he had to do to make his alchemy work was convince a railroad company to sacrifice

STREETER'S RAILROAD COLLISION.

DON'T MISS

STREETER'S

RAILROAD COLLISION!

A genuine collision between two 50-ton locomotives.

At 104th-st. Station,

ILLINOIS CENTRAL,

TODAY,

4 P. M.

LAST TIME IN CHICAGO.

Suburban and Special Express Trains every few minutes after 1:30. Last train at 3:30. Round trip and admission, 75c. Grand Stand.

ON PULLMAN ROAD RACE ROUTE.

Newspaper ad placed by the innovative if flawed Alfred L. Streeter touting the first-ever staged locomotive crash. *Author's collection.*

two obsolete engines otherwise destined for the salvage yards by running them together with throttles wide-open—that and promote the spectacle and collect money from an obviously thrill-thirsty public.

Streeter later told a newspaper reporter how he came by the idea. Rather than quote him directly, the journalist chose to summarize:

When clearing up wrecks…he observed with what eagerness all classes of people crowd about to get a view of…a thrilling accident, and from this he reasoned that people would be curious to see the result of two large engines pitted against each other. He did not have the money to back the project then but kept the idea in view until he felt in shape to carry it out.

Opportunity of a Lifetime

—TO VISIT A—

"Railway Collision!"

Between Two Forty-Ten Locomotives,

Each hauling a train of four cars, starting one
mile and a half apart, and coming together on a
track laid for the purpose in front of........

Buckeye Park, Saturday May 30, 1896.

At 3 o'clock, p. m. The most expensive, gigantic and realistic entertainment ever provided for the American people. Ample train service. Low excursion rates. Positively no postponement—rain or shine. under the management of W. H. FISHER, General Passenger and Ticket Agent and A. L. STREETER. Trains will leave Logan at 6:58 a. m., and 12:30 p. m. Round trip fare 75c, children 40c. Admission to Park Free.

Alfred Streeter widely
and dramatically
advertised his coming
pay-to-view crash,
an "Opportunity of
a Lifetime to Visit a
'Railway Collision!'"
Author's collection.

In the late spring of 1895, Streeter began working to set up a locomotive collision near Canton, Ohio, a railroad town in the northeastern part of the Buckeye State about sixty miles south of Cleveland. Whether he still held a traditional job is not known. He could have been one of the thousands of workers who had been laid off thanks to the nation's ongoing financial woes. But with the help of financial backers to whom he promised a piece of the action, and some money of his own, he leased acreage from a Stark County farmer and negotiated with the Cleveland, Canton & Southern Railroad to buy two old engines for a final run, one that would end with the opposing forty-ton locomotives crashing together at sixty miles per hour.

"It will be a show of an unusual kind," the *Akron Beacon Journal* said on June 13, 1895. "Sitting at a safe distance spectators will see two engines come together with all the force and terrific destructive effect of a railroad horror."

At a cost of $470, Streeter had overseen the decoration of the two doomed engines, a large locomotive painted red, white and blue and named "Protection" and a smaller engine named "Free Trade." For its less astute readers, the Akron newspaper pointed out the seemingly obvious, which was that "the engines are styled after the two political questions of the day." Gold versus silver was the larger national issue, but turmoil over tariffs ranked a close second. Each issue centered on the poor economy and how it might be improved with a change in national policy.

Streeter obviously hoped that his unique idea would be highly beneficial to his own economy, but it wasn't going to be easy. On July 18, only two days before his "great exhibition," the *Canton Repository* published a letter from Streeter headed "A Few Facts." It probably was paid for by Streeter, but that wasn't made clear in the newspaper. What was evident was his concern that the public misunderstood the coming event.

In a well-written brief that shows he had an education, Streeter said his planned collision was not a political "scheme" and that real locomotives would be used, not mock-ups as some people were saying. Nor were the engines merely discarded pieces of junk. He said they had been, in the railroad speak of the day, "shopped for repairs," but he had paid to have them put in top running order. Each of the eighty-thousand-pound machines was well capable of going sixty miles per hour. Anyone doubting that could come inspect them, he said. Finally, he sought to allay any safety concerns prospective ticket buyers might have. "Having had sixteen years' experience in the railway service in various capacities," he wrote, and "with the usual amount of accidents, enables me to say that there is positively no danger connected with this exhibition."

The collision was set for 3:00 p.m. Saturday, July 20, but in a figurative sense, the two trains destined for destruction never left the station. At the last minute, even though an estimated six thousand people had shown up to see the crash, the much-ballyhooed event got derailed.

"They are robbing me," Streeter told a *Canton Repository* reporter as he watched hundreds of people skirting the ticket booth to gather at a vantage point in the woods on the other side of the temporary tracks laid for the event. On top of that, the freeloaders had congregated too close to the planned point of impact. The frustrated promoter later said he had tried to get the people to move back but could not cajole the crowd to budge. Proceeding with the exhibition, he said, would not have been safe.

The railroad offered a different take on the last-minute cancellation. Streeter had not paid the $2,407.22 he owed for the locomotives.

Apparently, he had planned to pay the railroad from ticket sales, but because of the gate-crashers, not enough people had ponied up the $0.75 for him to be able to do that.

Later that day, a *Repository* reporter found a morose Streeter back in town. "He was very much depressed by the failure of his pet scheme," the reporter noted. Streeter said he had lost $1,800 "in hard cash," not counting what he owed. Still, he believed his idea would have worked if people hadn't tried to crash the crash. He was thinking about trying it again, possibly on Labor Day—this time with better fencing.

Referring to Streeter's pay-from-the-proceeds approach, the *Stark County Democrat* said, "Streeter had no right to arrange for such an affair in such a way. A number of people…traveled many miles bringing their families. Of course they were sore and mad and had a right to be. When a man gets up such an exhibition, he ought to have funds enough at hand to carry the thing through, whether there are 10 or 10,000 people there."

Streeter eventually decided against another attempt near Canton, opting for a site nearer a larger city. The following spring, apparently with new silent partner backing, he began talking with the Columbus, Hocking Valley & Toledo Railroad about staging a crash near Lancaster, Ohio, at Buckeye Park. The railroad had developed the recreational destination in 1891, hoping to lure Columbus residents and others to ride the CHV&T down to the park on weekends and holidays. Located twenty-six miles south of the capital city, the park featured a man-made lake for boaters and swimmers, a playground and other appealing amenities. This time, the railroader turned promoter got the railroad to donate two obsolete forty-ton engines for the nation's first-ever destruction derby. Not only would the railroad be furnishing the rolling stock, but the CHV&T would also lay the siding on which the collision would occur.

For his part, Streeter placed newspaper ads and distributed posters touting the coming crash, which one newspaper dubbed a "Railroad Wreck Made to Order." Streeter would make his money on the gate, while the railroad would profit in increased ticket sales and what would later be called "brand awareness."

Ads in Ohio newspapers extolled an "Opportunity of a Lifetime" to see a "Railway Collision!" They featured an engraving of two steam locomotives, each blowing black smoke, charging toward each other only moments before impact. Both engines, the ad continued, would be pulling four cars and meet at a point 1.5 miles from where they started. The collision would be "[t]he most expensive, gigantic and realistic entertainment ever provided for the American

This drawing depicting the May 30, 1896 "Duel of Locomotives" at Buckeye Park in Ohio accompanied a feature article on the smashup published in the *New York World*. *Author's collection.*

people." Round-trip tickets from anywhere on the CHV&T system would be seventy-five cents for adults and forty cents for children.

"The old engines were selected to end their days of usefulness before a concourse of pleasure seekers," one newspaper reported in advance of the Ohio event. The railroad had picked two aged engines that had been in use since the opening of the line a dozen years earlier.

As he had done before the failed Canton crash, Streeter paid to have the engines repainted "and decked in gala attire." The tender of one of the locomotives was labeled "W.H. Fisher" for the railroad's general passenger and ticket agent. This time, rather than further the name recognition of some national political figure, Streeter had his own name painted on the tender of the other doomed engine.

After the cars had been gussied up, the railroad put them on tour, hoping to attract a larger crowd for the big event. That happened on Saturday, May 9, with engines Number 12 and 21 steaming from Columbus via Marion to Toledo and then back. At the throttle of each locomotive was the veteran engineer who had been running the engine for years. Both men would get to start their old friends on their final trip in a few weeks. Referring to the decorated locomotives as "the leading characters in a [coming] mechanical tragedy," a writer for the *Marion Star* had opined on May 6, "It rather appalls one to think of the two great engines—such admirable creatures of iron and steel—being out for an airing in preparation for their day of execution, but one's curiosity grows in thinking of it."

Although the ads Streeter placed promised that each locomotive would be hauling four cars, on the day of the event, only three box cars and an old caboose were coupled behind each engine. They had been loaded with coal to add enough weight to make the collision as realistic as possible.

To Streeter's great satisfaction, people descended on Buckeye Park like a dumped load of coal. "Every train arriving…was loaded down with humanity and every vehicle owned within a radius of 20 miles was used to convey the curious to the place," the *Lancaster Daily Eagle* reported. People also came from the capital in city carriages and bicycles down the Columbus Pike.

With an estimated twenty to twenty-five thousand people looking on, the engineer in charge of each train backed up until the two locomotives were separated by about a mile and a half. Someone touched off a "bomb" (basically a large firecracker) and the engineers throttled up to about 10 miles an hour. At that point, they pulled their respective levers all the way back and jumped off the train. "At every revolution of the driving wheels the engines gained speed," the newspaper said, and by the time of impact they had reached the promised 50 miles an hour, 1.2 miles a minute.

One of many journalists on hand to cover the first-of-its kind event was Clarence Metters, who wrote a story on the crash for *National Magazine*. "Twenty-five thousand pairs of eyes were riveted upon one engine or the other as they rushed together," he wrote, "and so critical was the moment that scarcely a word was spoken. On and on sped the two iron monsters…."

Since one of the engines traveled a decided downgrade, it might have been moving even faster. That resulted in the collision happening about fifty yards from where Streeter and railroad officials had figured it would, but that caused no significant problems.

If Streeter somewhat miscalculated the point of impact, he was spot on in his showmanship. The Chicagoan had placed life-like dummies in the cab of each doomed locomotive and dressed them in regulation engineer's garb. Metters noted that "[m]ore than one woman covered her eyes, dreading to see the monsters come together, feeling that the trainmen had failed to get off in time, and that they were being carried to a certain and swift destruction."

Even the promoter and the railroad's management understood that they had to stay at least somewhat within the boundaries of safety and taste. That's why the railroad turned down one man's stupefying offer to ride one of the doomed trains to the point of impact in consideration of $1,500. He even said he would release the company from any liability.

Happening "quicker than thought," the resulting crash was terrific. "As the two iron monsters struck they rose in the air like stallions fighting and then crashed together so compactly that it was difficult to tell which engine was which," one reporter wrote. Escaping steam and smoke filled the air as the locomotives ground each other apart. "There was a terrific crash and a roar of escaping steam as the engines came together and they reared up in the air," an article in the *Salt Lake Tribune* reported. "The cars behind them were telescoped."

Ropes had been strung to keep the spectators at a safe distance, but a group of railroad workers, and likely Streeter and his helpers, stood only two hundred feet from the impact point. "Two flying pieces of iron came whistling through the air, and one struck Thomas G. Peck, chief clerk in the passenger department, breaking both bones of the left leg below the knee," one of the newspapers reported.

Meanwhile, the crowd stampeded through the barriers and rushed toward the wreckage. With upside-down drive wheels still spinning, "relic hunters began removing pieces of the broken machinery as souvenirs and soon the engines were dismantled." Indeed, the newspaper account continued, "Every bit of metal small enough to be portable was carried away by the enthusiastic spectators, who yelled themselves hoarse over the success of the entertainment."

Even if Streeter or the reporters covering the event exaggerated the size of the crowd, allowing for a 20 percent fudge factor, Streeter likely grossed $4,000 to $8,000—a tidy sum for the day. And this time, he and the railroad got box car loads of free publicity.

One of the journalists present for the event wrote a long story for the *New York World*. The piece, covering half a page, appeared with dramatic woodcut illustrations depicting the Ohio train crash. Newspapers all over the nation either reprinted the story or cribbed from it. What the journalist did not point out was that the event had been the first-known staged railroad crash in America, if not the world.

"The collision, which was the most expensive entertainment ever provided for an Ohio audience, was a tremendous success in every way," another newspaper said. Of course, it hadn't turned out all that well for the railroad

Wreckage showing remains of locomotive named "A.L. Streeter" at Buckeye Park south of Columbus, Ohio. *Author's collection.*

man who suffered a broken leg, but if that caused Streeter any regret, he got over it while counting his money.

Streeter had not been the only person to make money off the crash. To cater to those who had not brought their own food and beverages, a food stand operator sold sandwiches and coffee. In two hours, the vendor went through 400 loaves of bread and 2,100 buns. Clearly, putting on a locomotive crash amounted to opening a money factory—if done right.

The made-to-order crash, the *Chicago Tribune* said on June 2, was "comparable with nothing that has ever been offered to the public, and the thrill it caused is equally alone by its novel character." Some witnesses, the newspaper continued, had not been able to stand the tension as the two locomotives raced toward each other. "One Ohio citizen fell in a violent fit just as the great armored combatants dashed together."

Flush with success, Streeter began planning a second train crash for the upcoming Fourth of July holiday. This time it would be in Illinois. He chose Cicero, a community of some ten thousand residents, located over eight miles from Chicago.

The Independence Day event did not inspire much newspaper coverage, but it proved a literal smashing success. Newspapers reported that an estimated twenty-five thousand people turned out to witness the spectacle. The show began two and a half hours late, but the crowd got its money's worth as "the iron steeds dashed into each other while speeding along at forty-five miles an hour," the *Chicago Inter Ocean* reported on July 5. Both locomotives were "completely demolished," and all but one of the cars were "thrown off the track and badly damaged."

"The smashup," the newspaper continued, "was…gotten up by Mr. A.L. Streeter, both for the purpose of showing the curious how a couple of trains appeared after crashing into each other, and secondly in order that he might reap a few dollars, standard or otherwise. It is to his credit to say that he accomplished both purposes."

Based on the favorable outcome of the Cicero event, which considering the reported attendance may have yielded his biggest gross yet, Streeter decided to go to the figurative water tank once more. By trial and error he had learned the importance of access control in ensuring that everyone who saw the wreck had paid to do so. But this time he encountered a new problem: bureaucratic red tape.

As the *Chicago Tribune* revealed, "The managers experienced considerable trouble in getting a permit to hold the show inside…the city limits, but the officials of the operating department of the Illinois Central gave the Chief of Police assurances which were satisfactory that there was no possible danger of an explosion or other mishap, and on that assurance he issued the permit."

The permit issue resolved, Streeter oversaw the building of a temporary park suitable to accommodate a large crowd. The venue was off 104th Street, just below Burnside and not far from the giant Pullman Company plant. One of the people who would pay a half dollar to see the event described the scene: "An immense canvas on poles was stretched around some 10 or 15 acres…taking in a single track, comfortable seats being provided on the inside. At either end of the track was a gate, also made of canvas."

Streeter had the engines selected by the railroad "painted to present a nice appearance." In addition to giving each engine a fresh coat of paint, Streeter had one locomotive labeled "Gold Standard," with the other one named "Free Silver." To add to the joke, the cab of one engine was labeled "McKinley" and the other "Bryan." As a final touch, the headlamp of each locomotive bore a large portrait of each politician. When it came time for the crash, each engine would be pulling three box cars.

Although the planned smashup was all about making money for Streeter and the railroad, the *Tribune* disingenuously labeled the event an "attempt to divert the public for a few hours from the incessant din of a political wrangle by furnishing a sort of counter-irritant."

People began arriving by train on the seventeenth for the July 18 event. The early birds got to see the moribund engines make a trial run, but the scheduled show had to be canceled because of heavy rain. When the event finally came off on July 25, the postponement seems to have had an adverse impact on the gate. This time, just seven thousand people showed up.

Someone identified only as "A Spectator" sent an account of Streeter's second Chicago-area crash to the *Alton (IL) Telegraph*:

> *At the appointed hour two engines were backed away from the meeting place until about a mile apart. At a given signal the throttles were thrown wide open, the engineers jumped from their positions and the engines started on their last trip with a leap. On and on they came like two mad demons, every moment with increased speed, until in the center of the arena, they met with a terrific crash that could be heard for miles around. The debris was piled twenty feet in the air while flying particles ascended as high as seventy-five feet. Immediately a rush was made by the crowd toward the wreck to procure some particle of it as a memento of the occasion. Nobody was hurt.*

If the crowd estimate was accurate, and assuming most of them paid to see the crash, Streeter would have grossed roughly $3,500. Unfortunately for the innovative promoter, most of that cash went up in steam. The promoter had borrowed front money from a man named A.C. McCord. For reasons not explained in the newspapers, McCord had grown nervous about the prospect of being repaid. As Streeter busied himself supervising things before the crash, a Cooke County sheriff's deputy showed up to serve him notice that his money man had on the previous day obtained a $2,732 judgment against Streeter. The court order gave the deputy authority to seize enough of the exhibition's proceeds to satisfy that judgment.

The Chicagoan who had staged the nation's first pay-to-see train wreck may have gone on to promote as many as seven collisions, but only five are documented. Streeter put on a crash at Evansville, Indiana, on September 27 that year, and the Columbus *Ohio State Journal* reported that Streeter oversaw another crash in the Buckeye State on May 28, 1898. If he did, no other newspaper in the state mentioned it. The Spanish-American War was in progress, and the conflict dominated the headlines.

However many locomotive crashes he produced, one thing is certain: Alfred Streeter had invented a new form of entertainment, in the process developing a business model. And with attention to detail and a measure of good luck he could generate a nice return on the investment. Streeter would become a millionaire, but not from promoting locomotive collisions. And despite his future success, his reputation—and his fortune—would end in a figurative train wreck of his own doing.

A MAN WITH A VERY APROPOS NAME

When William George Crush moved to Texas from Kentucky to go to work for the MKT, it didn't take long before friends and colleagues took to calling him "Colonel Crush." He had no military background and hadn't yet turned thirty, but folks who knew of his Blue Grass State origin thought it fitting to insert the southern honorific in front of his name. What they didn't know was that Crush wasn't his real last name.

Born to Charles and Christine Krusch on July 3, 1865, only a few months after the end of the Civil War, Billie (as his family and friends called him) grew up in his native Louisville, Kentucky. Although several battles and skirmishes had been fought in the vicinity of Louisville, the Blue Grass State's largest city had remained firmly in Union control and unscathed by the bloody four-year war between the states. In the postwar period during which Billie grew up, the Ohio River town emerged as one of the principle cities of the central South.

When interviewed by a federal census enumerator in 1870, Charles Krusch, a German immigrant whose wife was originally from Tennessee, said he was thirty-five and listed his occupation as "merchant tailor." He and his wife had four children—three boys and one girl—ranging in age from seven to one. Billie was the oldest son, a year younger than his big sister, Anna.

A decade later, still living in Louisville, the family had grown. Billie had three more brothers and a baby sister only six months old. But something else involving the family had changed as well. When federal head counters

Newspaper engraving depicting Katy general passenger agent William G. Crush about the time of the Crash at Crush. *Author's collection.*

canvassed Louisville for the 1880 census, the family's last name went on the rolls as Crush. For whatever reason, Charles Krusch had chosen to Anglicize his last name, not an uncommon practice at the time among American families with immigrant roots.

Likely neither Billie nor anyone else in his family gave any thought to possessing a last name that was both a proper noun and a verb, but the uncommon surname would one day make for an irresistible play on words for journalists. A cynic might even suspect that Billie Crush had changed his name in his early thirties to fit a particular circumstance, but he had nothing to do with it. He did, however, sometimes add a day to his age, telling reporters he was born on Independence Day, not the day before.

Although Louisville had a population of more than 120,000 in 1880, Crush attended St. Xavier's College (now Xavier University) in Cincinnati, Ohio. Founded in 1831 as the Athenaeum, it was the first Catholic college in Ohio and the sixth oldest in the nation. An all-male institution that also included a high school, St. Xavier offered two basic educational paths: a general education in all the standard disciplines with strong emphasis on the classics or a curriculum that would prepare a student for a career in business. He probably took some business courses, but he did not get a degree there.

In the nineteenth century, many an oldest son chose to follow his father's line of work, but not Crush. At eighteen, he opted to become a railroad man. That happened on August 1, 1883, when he went on the payroll of the Louisville, New Albany & Chicago Railroad (known to travelers and employees alike as the "Monon Route") as a clerk in the company's auditing department in Louisville.

The same day young Crush began his railroad career, President Chester A. Arthur was in town for the opening ceremonies of the Southern Exposition, a world's fair–level industrial and merchandising show that would run for one hundred days. The event, held annually for the next four years, brought tens of thousands of visitors to Louisville, most of them by rail. That a notable attraction of some sort was good for railroad business was not lost on the young Kentuckian.

Crush's first increase in responsibility and salary involved a move to Chicago, where he worked as a rate clerk in the Monon's general passenger agent's office. At the company's end-of-the-line facility, he got promoted to the position of traveling passenger agent before returning to Louisville in the mid-summer of 1888 as the company's district passenger agent.

In the summer of 1893, now twenty-eight with nearly a decade of white-collar railroad experience, Crush left the Monon to become general passenger agent for the MKT in Texas effective August 1. At the time, the Katy had its headquarters in Denison, and that's where Crush moved.

W. G. CRUSH, PASSENGER TRAFFIC MANAGER

Crush photo from the *MKT Employee Magazine* in 1916. *Author's collection.*

He joined the Katy, as a profile on him in the *MKT Employee Magazine* later put it, "young, alert, vigorous and dynamic." Crush knew, the unnamed company writer continued, "the mechanics of the game, and had definite ideas about the promotion of passenger business."

The first idea Crush came up with to drum up business for the Katy involved capitalizing on the World's Fair in Chicago, which had opened that May. Crush offered special fares on the newly begun Katy Flyer, a premier passenger train that ran through Texas to Kansas City and St. Louis. The railroad had showed off the train at the MKT Depot in Fort Worth on June 13, 1893. "Everything about it [the Flyer] is the perfection of art and ingenuity, from the plate glass mirrors to the hammered brass hand rails," the *Fort Worth Gazette* gushed. The coach cars were of the latest vestibule-type design with reclining seats that, unlike on some lines, did not cost extra. In addition, the train would include at least one Wagner Palace sleeping car, a luxurious piece of rolling stock considered even more comfortable than Pullman cars. Another amenity was that all the passenger cars were illuminated at night by gas lights. The following day, the Flyer pulled out for the MKT station in Dallas and then continued down the line, with viewing stops at Waxahachie, Hillsboro, Waco and, finally, Houston. From the Bayou City, the train made its first northbound trip with paying passengers, many of them headed for the fair in Chicago.

While the MKT had decided to launch the luxury train before Crush started as general passenger agent, he did all he could to tout its comfort, convenience and table fare. "[T]he records show that [Crush's] originality, enterprise and versatility soon had it the best known train in the country," the Katy's in-house magazine later boasted. Other railroads would disagree that the Katy had either the best or the best-known premier train, but the Flyer certainly ranked as one of the nation's top named passenger trains.

The Katy continued to get its money's worth out of Crush during his first year on the job. Having enhanced his company's bottom line with World's Fair–related ticket sales, the new general passenger agent turned his attention to the thriving coastal city of Galveston and began promoting the island as an attractive recreational destination via the Katy. On September 23, 1893, scores of special Katy trains carried ten thousand "excursionists" to Galveston, a visit arranged by Crush with cheerful assistance from local officials and businessmen. The Katy promoter had offered a four-dollar round-trip excursion rate from anywhere on the line's system, good for one week. The result was a veritable flood of visitors descending on Galveston, temporarily increasing its population by roughly one-third.

Galveston's economic mainstay was its busy port, where dock workers loaded more outbound cotton bales onto freighters than anywhere else in the world. But as a popular chamber of commerce saying held, "A tourist is a whole lot easier to pick than a bale of cotton." To that end, the city offered visitors a long, breezy beach on the Gulf of Mexico, nice hotels, fine eating places and first-rate entertainment venues. Beyond that, the Oleander City had wide-open gambling and prostitution. Those who haughtily held themselves out as "B.O.I." (Born on the Island) saw Galveston more as a sovereign city-state than a part of Texas.

In appreciation of Crush's efforts to make Galveston a popular destination for railroad travelers, on October 4 a grateful business community presented him with an expensive diamond pin at a banquet replete with fresh oysters and Gulf seafood. Not only had Crush lured thousands of visitors and their money (then often referred to as "railroad dollars") to the island city, but the MKT was also practically ignoring Galveston's chief rival, Houston. Occasionally, the Katy even thumbed its corporate nose at the Bayou City and ran trains through to Galveston without stopping in Houston. That, the *St. Louis Post-Dispatch* reported, had resulted in "considerable jealousy…between Houston and Galveston, which promises to terminate in interesting developments."

(Houston would continue to play second fiddle to Galveston economically until oil was discovered in southeast Texas in 1901 and Houston got its own deep-water port in 1914. The killer hurricane of September 8, 1900, added to the island city's woes.)

Four years after Crush accepted a diamond pin as a token of appreciation on the part of Galveston's movers and shakers, the *Houston Post* published a staff artist's engraving of him, along with a brief profile. The drawing clearly shows what may well be that same piece of jewelry shining just beneath the knot of his tie. Wearing a suit, vest and the high-collar white shirt of the day, Crush had a slightly receding hairline and a prominent nose beneath which hung a bushy mustache. He had a strong jaw line and jutting chin, with not even a hint of a smile showing above it. The newspaper cut reveals a handsome, well-groomed, successful and self-confident thirty-two-year-old railroad executive.

A longtime bachelor, Crush remained single until the spring of 1898. At the age of thirty-three, he married St. Louis native Katherine (Kay) Rosenbaum, in Philadelphia. Back in Texas after their honeymoon, on May 2, he and his twenty-eight-year-old wife made their home in ever-growing Dallas, where, much to the chagrin of Denison's business community, the MKT had moved its headquarters in 1895.

The same year Crush started with the Katy, the national economy took a downturn that became a near freefall. Fortunate to even have a job, Crush saw the Katy struggling to stay solvent. By 1894, the situation had worsened to the extent that the MKT began laying off employees and even shuttering some of its offices.

"General Passenger Agent W.G. Crush of the Missouri, Kansas and Texas railway and Traveling Auditor J. Lisk…arrived here yesterday morning for the purpose of checking up the Galveston city office in charge of Mr. Hiram A. Johnson," the *Galveston News* reported on January 20, 1894. By "checking up," the newspaper meant auditing and closing out the office's financial account preparatory to shutting down the office. Johnson, the article continued, would be transferred to a newly opened MKT office in San Antonio. The closure of the Galveston office had as much to do with a court case that had, for the time being, barred MKT from running trains to the island city than it did the company's financial health, but it would save a little money until it reopened.

Later that month, the Katy's worried general manager, A.A. Allen, ordered a payroll reduction of ten dollars per day for each employee. On February 3, the railroad let go "a number" of machinists, blacksmiths and laborers at its normally busy Denison facilities with, as the *Denison Herald* reported on February 7, "prospects of further reduction in the next few days." The issue, the newspaper continued, was "due to slack business, which the Katy has been experiencing lately."

Despite the poor economy, the MKT did better than many other railroads. By the time the financial situation improved, a quarter of the nation's railroads had shut down. The Katy survived through belt-tightening, good management and, arguably, the efforts of its energetic general passenger agent.

The January 1891 issue of *Railway Agent and Station Agent*, a trade magazine published in Cleveland, reprinted a humorous but not-far-off-the-mark description of a general passenger agent:

> *The general passenger agent is the most important man on the railroad, at least those who ask favors of him think so. The gpa is a man of varied attainments. Acknowledging the press as the most mighty power of the nineteenth century, he stands in with the editor. With profound respect for the church as the guide and teacher of the world, he makes reduced rates for the clergy and runs excursions for the Sunday school for almost nothing…*
>
> *His duties are as varied and as arduous as there are days in the month. On Sunday he must attend church to prove that the railroads set a good example to the community. Monday night he must take a party of ticket agents to the theatre and show them about town in order that they may be impressed with the liberality of the company, and in the hope that they will send their business over his line. At an early hour on the following morning he must meet the general manager at the office to discuss plans for the reduction of expenses. Wednesday he must convince the advertising agent of each of the daily papers that he is paying him more money for time tables and reading notices than any other paper in the country. Thursday he devotes to trying to get a lot of reading notices into the papers free—upon the plea that they are really items of news. Friday he spends in making a map that shows his line the shortest and most direct to every important point in the United States. Saturday he makes out a time table that no one but the maker can read. He goes home Saturday night with the proud consciousness that he has done a splendid week's work and earned his princely salary.*

Before press agentry morphed into the field of public relations, passenger agents and traveling passenger agents handled a railroad line's promotional efforts. Their primary job was to get tickets sold, and to that end, they did all they could to generate human and freight traffic for their company. What was good for the railroads often was good for a particular community. In his 1948 history of the Katy, author Vincent Victor Masterson, himself a former MKT public relations man, called Crush "the Katy's first great press agent."

While the Katy would not have direct service through Austin until 1904, the MKT's mainline lay only thirty miles from the capital, and it was easy enough to run special trains through track usage agreements with other lines. So when a dam across the Colorado River created Texas's first large man-made lake in the spring of 1893, Crush helped organize an international rowing regatta that was held on the impoundment, named Lake McDonald after the mayor who pushed for its construction.

Working with Waco officials in 1894, Crush had significant input in the development of Waco's Cotton Palace. That fall, multiple thousands of people traveled on the Katy and other lines to visit the exposition, which one visitor said topped the Chicago World's Fair. While that was a bit over the top, the event was considered a huge success, and all concerned were looking forward to an even bigger and better exposition the following year and in years to come. Unfortunately, the ornate, all-wood Victorian exhibition hall burned down in January 1895. Crush also was credited with playing a significant role in the creation of San Antonio's annual Battle of the Flowers and San Jacinto Fiesta, an event that continues into the twenty-first century.

One way to get your employer's name in the newspapers is to be friendly with reporters, and being an affable man with the authority to issue free passes, as well as an expense account for buying people lunch, that came easy for Crush. Journalists also appreciated a corporate official not only unafraid to go on the record but also who said things well. In the jargon of the Fourth Estate, he "made good copy." Newspaper publishers mindful of the business side of things appreciated something else about Crush: he handled the Katy's advertising buys.

An example of Crush's popularity with the press is an article in the June 10, 1894 edition of the *Denison Sunday Gazetteer* noting that the MKT general passenger agent was back in Galveston. "Mr. Crush says the Katy will run in here again at an early date, and when Mr. Crush says a thing you may count upon it as a certainty," the *Galveston Opera Glass* assured its readers.

When the Texas Press Association met at Waco's posh Pacific Hotel in May 1895 for its sixteenth annual convention, delegates were read a telegram from Crush "extending the courtesies of his road for an excursion to the [Confederate veterans] reunion in Houston." The courtesies extended were free round-trip passes on the MKT for newspaper publishers or editors. The minutes of the meeting, published in the *Fort Worth Gazette* of May 17, reflect that Crush's offer of free rides was graciously accepted by the membership.

The Katy executive must have had a scheduling conflict that prevented him from making a personal appearance at the convention to hand out the passes and hobnob with the gentlemen of the press, but no one minded. As the *Dallas Morning News* said of him, Crush was "a man who makes acquaintances rapidly and turns the majority into friendships."

Having good rapport with the press was to be desired, but in some cases, adverse publicity could not be avoided. Just after dark on Christmas Day 1894, a southbound MKT passenger train collided with a westbound Houston & Texas Central passenger train at a crossing near Waxahachie in Ellis County. Each train, the *Galveston News* reported, had been "heavily laden with passengers." Seventeen of those passengers were injured, two gravely.

The Houston & Texas Central train had stopped before the crossing, as per railroad procedure. The Katy engineer also knew that a crossing was coming up, but when he applied the air brakes, they did not work. Seeing the approach of the other train after he rounded a curve, he threw the engine into reverse, pulling the throttle back to full steam. Realizing that his train was going to crash into the other train, he and his fireman jumped from the locomotive at the last minute. Moments later, the engine smashed into one of the other train's rear passenger cars.

The Katy accident, serious as it was, proved minor in comparison to the July 30, 1896 crash of two passenger trains near Atlantic City, New Jersey, that claimed fifty lives and injured scores more. In the accident, a Reading Railroad express train slammed into a West Jersey Line excursion train pulling five coaches crowded with Improved Order of the Redmen conventioneers.

Crush pored over published accounts of that disaster and kept up with other railroad happenings in the newspapers and industry trade publications. He had a good education for the times, perhaps an even better imagination and a proven eye for paying attention to details.

"Crush is one of the fixtures of Dallas," the *Dallas Morning News* said of him. "He has done more through his own personality to advertise the Katy than many passenger agents have been able to do with the aid of folders and dodgers. He has been at the head of the passenger department of the Katy's big Texas system for years, and is better known, perhaps, than any other passenger traffic man in the State."

While his name frequently made the newspapers and appeared on a lot of the railroad's advertising, Crush still had people to whom he reported: "Although Mr. James Barker of St. Louis is above Mr. Crush in official position, he long ago learned that the [MKT] passenger department of Texas was in very capable hands, and let Mr. Crush run things to suit himself. The fact that when people travel the Katy gets its share and sometimes more of those going and coming is ample proof of the wisdom of Mr. Barker's course. Like all successful passenger agents, Mr. Crush believes in slinging printer's ink. In this he employs unique and original methods," the *Dallas Morning News* article noted.

Like a well-maintained steam locomotive with a full water tank and topped-off coal tender, in coming up with "unique and original methods" of ginning up business for his company, in the railroad language of the day Crush was about to highball it down the figurative tracks to a lasting place in American cultural history.

THE SINCEREST FORM OF FLATTERY

The August 5, 1896 edition of the *Dallas Morning News* included a brief but eye-catching news item from Waco: the MKT was "making preparations for a head-end collision of two passenger trains, to consist of a locomotive, a tender and six passenger coaches."

The Central Texas correspondent for the Dallas newspaper neglected to mention that no one would be riding in the trains when they crashed together, leaving readers to figure that out for themselves. Word of the upcoming event came, of course, from William G. Crush. The Katy's general passenger agent said that along with Waco passenger and ticket agent J.E. Smith, he had been out for two days looking for a "suitable point to make the test."

Test? Not until the *News*'s Waco man was halfway into his article did he explain that the collision was "designed to observe the effect of the running into each other of two passenger trains going at high speed." That, the journalist continued, "will disclose the points of greatest injury, the force such collisions cause and enable manufacturers of cars and locomotives to build with a view to reducing loss of life and property."

It sounded very high-minded—a railroad corporation so dedicated to passenger safety that even in tough economic times it was willing to sacrifice "good locomotives and cars" to better serve its customers. Several suitable spots for the "test" had been found, Crush said, and one of them, "somewhere between Hillsboro and Temple," would be chosen. However, he continued, the location would not be disclosed.

Downtown Waco around the beginning of the twentieth century. *Author's collection.*

What ticket agent Smith did not at all mind making public was that it would "be an appalling sight when the two trains rush into each other." Despite that, he added, "there have been applications for permission to ride in the rear cars made by parties willing to incur the danger for the sake of the excitement and the notoriety it will give them."

Crush and Smith made their comments on August 4. The day before, Crush had spoken with another reporter in Waxahachie, sixty-six miles north up the Katy line from Waco. Whether he had reached out to the scribe or whether the journalist had approached him is not known. However, back then newspaper editors tended to assign a reporter—often just a "cub"—to be at the local depot before each day's scheduled arrivals. It's likely the reporter's curiosity had been piqued when an engine pulling an MKT inspection car and what appeared to be some kind of work car hissed to a stop at the Waxahachie depot.

On board the special train, the young newsman soon learned, were Crush; O.B. Maer, superintendent of the MKT's southern division; and John Ringling of the Ringling Bros. Circus. "While the party was here [the correspondent] learned the object of this official visit," the unnamed reporter wrote. "Since the exposition collision of two trains in Ohio some months ago the railroad world has been looking forward to the time when another collision would be pulled off, where even a larger [crowd] than witnessed the first could be present, and where the importance of such a collision, with results, could be duly recorded and given out authentically."

Crush told the Waxahachie reporter that the collision would be held "near Waxahachie." Not only that, he added, but the railroad also expected as many as 100,000 people would show up to see the staged train wreck. If that attendance were realized, it would amount to one-fifth of the state's total population.

By all rights, word of such a planned event should have been page-one news, especially in Central Texas. But for whatever reason—possibly that the journalist's boss had taken Crush's comments either as exaggeration or a try at free advertising—the coming locomotive crash was relegated to a short back-page story. The presence of John Ringling should have been the first clue that there was more to the planned collision than a noble effort to improve railroad safety.

Ringling and four of his six brothers had been running their circus for a dozen years by this time, and each year the big show had become

Ringling Bros. Circus poster showing John Ringling, the promoter who coached William G. Crush on how to put on a big show. *Author's collection.*

bigger and more successful. His surname, just like "Barnum" and "Bailey," had become virtually synonymous with circus. The renowned showman's connection to the MKT was natural enough. Since the Ringlings had stopped traveling from venue to venue in a caravan of circus wagons in 1889, they had been using the rail lines. When the Ringling circus came to Texas, the MKT hauled the entertainment company's sixty rail cars. Since John Ringling was the show's advance man in charge of transportation and other arrangements, he and Crush became acquainted after Crush joined the Katy in 1893.

Whether in exchange for certain courtesies extended on the part of the Katy or purely in the spirit of friendship—all accounts have Crush being a hail fellow, well-met type—or simply for money, Ringling had agreed to tutor the Dallas railroad man on planning and promoting a really big show. In seeking Ringling's counsel, Crush could not have made a smarter choice. The thirty-year-old McGregor, Iowa native had started out as a clown, but soon he and his brothers hired others to be funnymen. John's true talent was in logistics, selecting towns to visit and handling the myriad tasks associated with moving hundreds of people and animals and all the necessary equipment from gig to gig.

The Katy special that stopped in Waxahachie that day also pulled what the circus trade called an advertising car. It was one of four then belonging to the Ringling company. Crush did not have enough of the details worked out for posters to have been printed yet, but circus hands traveling with Ringling were putting up wooden billboards along the Katy right of way that in a few weeks would host posters advertising the crash once the particulars had been determined.

In addition to his event planning expertise and assistance in the placing of billboards, Ringling had agreed to provide the railroad with one of its big white tents and the crew needed to put it up and take it down. Despite the tent's size, it could be put up or struck in only a few hours. In fact, a good crew could get one down and on the train for the next show in an hour.

Crush went on to tell the Waxahachie reporter that the tentative date for the crash was September 8, barely a month out. What they were looking for in a crash site was a spot offering two summer necessities: shade and water. Once a location had been selected, he continued, two engines, each pulling six cars, would be "allowed to collide while going a full speed." Of course, the Katy would be selling excursion tickets for the event. Either the railroad had not determined how much it would cost to travel to the crash venue or Crush decided to hold that back until more arrangements had been made.

Part of the date selection likely had to do with the Ringling Bros. Texas schedule. The circus would be opening in the state on September 26 at Gainesville, a town served by the MKT. From Cooke County, via the Katy, the show would travel to Dallas. From that city, it would play various other Texas towns through October 24. Obviously, Ringling would not want the Katy competing for the public's attention with his show.

The short story filed by the Waxahachie journalist left much unanswered, but it marked the first mention in print of what the Dallas-based passenger agent had in mind.

In January 1896—six months before Streeter staged his first crash—while traveling by rail from New York to St. Louis, Crush had experienced a train wreck firsthand when the engine blew up and the train detailed. The Katy official was not injured, but the incident made a definite impression. "There was no town nearby," he later recalled, "yet within probably thirty minutes, and certainly not more than an hour, hundreds of people had assembled at the scene. This occurred, too, long before the automobile, in the days overland transportation was slow, to say the least." That got Crush thinking.

"Reflecting on the crowd collected at the wreck and realizing curiosity was the impelling motive that had induced them to come," he said in the only interview he is known to have ever given following the wreck, the thought came to him: "If so many persons will gather at the scene of a wreck enduring, perhaps, great inconvenience to gratify their curiosity, what wouldn't they do to attend a railroad train wreck that had been deliberately planned? It was a thought that remained in my mind, for in addition to being in the nature of a scientific experiment, the publicity the railroad would receive was an element not to be overlooked. The more I reflected on the possibilities, the more feasible did the scheme appear."

Streeter's Memorial Day crash in Ohio likely solidified Crush's thinking. It's even possible he had been among the spectators at Buckeye Park that spring, but if he wasn't there, he definitely read newspaper accounts of the event. As a *Dallas Morning News* reporter later put it, the Katy official "thought it was a great scheme and that such an event in Texas would draw more than half as many people as it did in Ohio."

Crush's first thought was to do something different and derail a train at high speed, designing the wreck so that the locomotive and cars would crash into a bridge. But the more he mulled it over, crashing two engines head-to-head seemed like a better idea. "This decision reached, I recommended it to my superior officers," Crush said.

At first, despite Crush's previous promotional successes, the Katy's upper management did not share their general passenger agent's enthusiasm for such an exhibition on their line. "They were afraid the Texans would not give sufficient patronage to the show to pay for the wrecked rolling stock," the Dallas newspaper said.

Actually, the brass probably was more worried about the safety of spectators and the risk of litigation should anything go amiss. Crush persisted, telling the powers that were that he would "be willing to risk everything he had that the collision would draw very nearly as many people as one of the big attractions at the [Texas] state fair." Not only that, he continued, he was prepared to put his reputation on the line and "risk everything on the venture." If the management said yes, he promised to "make it a success or bust a trace chain [trying]."

Eventually, Crush's proposition was laid before New York–based MKT president Henry C. Rouse, a protégé of John D. Rockefeller's and the head of the Katy since 1891. Whether Rouse's opinion was solicited by mail or in person, possibly at a meeting at the company's St. Louis office, the millionaire Cleveland native whose passion was sailing his private yacht worried about the safety of spectators should he approve Crush's request.

Accordingly, Crush talked with several engineers at the company's busy Denison yard. The management's concern was that the impact of a head-on collision would rupture the two locomotive's high-pressure steam boilers.

HENRY C. ROUSE.

Newspaper engraving of Katy president Henry Rouse, the man who gave the final okay for the Crash at Crush. *Author's collection.*

The result of that would be a tremendous explosion. All but one of the veteran "hoggers" Crush consulted assured him that this would not happen. But an Irish Katy shop foreman named Hanrahan (his last name is not known) disagreed, warning that the boilers would burst and that there would be injuries. His fervor unabated, Crush decided to accept the majority opinion and reported back to his bosses that the collision could be safely staged. "Before such enthusiasm," the *Dallas Morning News* said, "nothing could stand long. Crush won his point."

On August 9, on the far southern end of the Katy line, the *Houston Post* ran a brief article headlined "The Katy Smashup."

1870s vintage locomotive similar to the two engines deleted from the MKT's rolling stock in the smashup north of Waco, Texas. *Author's collection.*

According to that item, "A good deal of interest is being awakened in the projected train wreck which the Katy is said to have determined upon."

The phrase "public relations" had not yet come into usage, but Crush clearly had a good instinct for building a proper image for his company. The Houston newspaper's blurb noted that the crash would be "for the benefit of science" as well as for the public's entertainment. Houston's Katy ticket agent told the Bayou City journalist that the coming train collision "is going to eclipse anything of the kind ever attempted." So that people could enjoy the spectacle, he continued, the Katy would be offering special excursion rates "from all points on the road."

Meanwhile, Crush worked faster than the speedy Katy Flyer to get the word out. As the *Dallas Morning News* later told its readers, "He advertised [the collision] from ocean to ocean. He put notices in every paper in the state. He got other roads [railroad companies] interested. He got out fine lithographs showing the terrible damage that was going to be done. He issued circulars. Nothing was left undone. No avenue whereby his scheme could be pushed was neglected."

Crush's publicity campaign had one unexpected, and problematic, consequence: a sustained barrage of correspondence. People wanted more details on the coming event. Political candidates sought permission to speak to the crowd. Others wanted to set up sales stands. Reporters wanted assurances of an advantageous vantage point from which to view the crash. And, of course, they would like to have free passes.

The letters came slowly at first, no more than a few per day. Then Crush's in-basket began filling with a dozen letters with each day's delivery. Soon he was getting twenty letters daily, some from as far west as the Pacific coast, others even from the Far East. "Finally," the *Dallas Morning News* said, "he received so many that he found it absolutely impossible, even with three stenographers, to begin to answer his collision correspondence alone."

That figurative runaway mail train coming in response to the publicity he had generated convinced Crush that he was on track for a huge crowd. And except for locals who could travel by foot, horse, wagon or bicycle, most of the spectators would have purchased train tickets from the Katy.

By mid-August, Crush's plan had solidified. A *Dallas Morning News* reporter who interviewed him said that Crush had "nothing on his mind…save a grand scientific show he is preparing for men of all political parties. He doesn't know anything else, he doesn't think anything else, he can't talk about anything else, and won't." Crush and the nameless reporter clearly had fun with the interview.

"Oh, but it's going to be a smashup," said the Katy passenger agent.

"What is," the journalist asked. "The Republican convention at Fort Worth?"

"Republican convention? No!" Crush shouted.

Following that came a figurative runaway freight train of "gasping, exclamatory explanations, from which the reporter learned that Crush had nearly perfected arrangements for the great locomotive collision exhibition, which is to be given soon in the interest of science." Obviously, Crush intended to stick to his story that the crash would be beneficial for man's greater understanding of engineering and physics, not an event whose primary purpose was to improve the Katy's cash flow. And the reporter did not question that.

The railroad reporter for the *Dallas Times-Herald*, the *Morning News'* afternoon competitor, button-holed Crush about the coming event. "Yes, I have found a location," he told the reporter, who referred to him as Billy Crush. "It's a beaut, too, and looks like it had been designed especially for the Katy's benefit." Crush couldn't tell the *Times-Herald* journalist exactly where the crash would be staged, but he was free with other particulars: engines pulling six cars each would start two miles apart "that they may gain a speed of 60 or 65 miles an hour before coming together." The site selected "will hold 250,000 persons." Fifty excursion trains, he continued, "will unload big loads there....It will be a great smash-up, something exciting and interesting."

Several factors played into the site selection. First, the location was roughly at the midpoint of the company's Texas mileage; second, the spot— at Katy mile marker 831—was only three miles south of the West depot and fourteen miles north of Waco. At the time, served by the Katy and five other railroads, Waco was Texas's eighth-largest city with more than twenty thousand residents. Only thirty-five miles south of Waco was Temple, a division point on the Atchison, Topeka & Santa Fe Railroad with some seven thousand residents. Nearby Belton had another three thousand–plus people living there. Hillsboro, thirty-three miles north of Waco, had another five thousand in population, and Waxahachie, sixty-six miles to the north, had some four thousand residents. That meant more than thirty-nine thousand people lived well inside a two-hour train ride of the crash site. Another sixty-one thousand–plus people lived in the Dallas–Fort Worth area, and fifteen thousand–plus in Austin, all within one hundred miles of Waco.

Another important determinant in site selection had to do with topography. Crush told the *Dallas Times-Herald* that the spot was "a natural amphitheater," with high ground on either side of the Katy mainline. "All [spectators] will be in full view of the track," he added.

The railroad leased acreage from landowners on both sides of its right of way—J.B. Dickenson on the west side and John Foit on the east side— for a distance of three miles. The largest portion of the lease lay on the west side of the tracks, with the area to be set aside for infrastructure and the crowd being one hundred acres. That would make it about one-tenth the size of New York's Central Park. Planning for the crash to occur in the late afternoon, Crush realized that the majority of the spectators would be able to stand on the higher western hillside with the sun to their backs. The width of the swath was not reported, but one later account mentioned that some of the spectators on the west side stood one thousand feet from the rails. Not only did the farmers get money for making part of their property available to the railroad, on the assumption that the horde expected to see the crash would be trampling the farmer's crops, but the company also bought what the landowners had been growing.

"Do you fear that the governor will call a special session to prevent the mill?" the *Dallas Morning News* reporter had asked Crush, wondering if the state would try to block the event as it had the Fitzsimmons-Maher prizefight earlier that year.

"No, no," Crush replied. "We expect to invite him to see it—all in the interest of science, you know. There will be no harm done save the smashing to pieces of two 40-ton passenger engines, a dozen cars and the tearing up of several hundred yards of track and roadbed. The engines will be used for scrap iron if they are damaged beyond repair, and the track will be cleared and mended in a jiffy."

Back to his for-the-sake-of-science gambit, Crush said railroad men "from all over the west" would be on hand to see the crash and that "photographic observations will be taken every second for ten seconds before the collision." He said railroad industry manufacturers were "deeply interested in furnishing engines with appliances which will lessen the shock of collisions, and consequently make them less dangerous to human life." The Katy's crash, he went on, "will undoubtedly prove of great value to railroad mechanics, in that they will get valuable suggestions."

Crush may have actually believed what he was saying. On the other hand, he clearly was getting caught up in his figurative carnival barking. The potential crowd had already grown in Crush's public comments from 100,000 to 250,000. Maybe he only meant that there would be room at the site for that many people should they opt to see the crash, but what he said gave people the impression that practically everyone in Texas planned on seeing the spectacle.

At this point in the interview, the *Morning News* reporter said, "It is to be a public exhibition, of course?" Yes, Crush replied. Public interest had been high ever since word of the planned event got out, he said. In fact, he continued, "in order to let all see it we will run excursions from all along our lines at low rates, say less than one fare for the round trip."

And wait, there was more. "The large number of people who will be present will furnish a good opportunity for politicians to expound their doctrines, and we shall invite representative men of all parties to be present and address the people," he said. Contradicting himself on his earlier declared crowd estimates, Crush said that "from all indications" fifteen to twenty thousand people would be on hand to see the exhibition.

Nor did the Katy intend for all those people, and hopefully more, to be in any way uncomfortable or bored. "There will be plenty to eat, and if a man really pines for red lemonade he can get it." Not only that, he went on, "There will be 'flying jennies,' shooting galleries, targets and other forms of amusement, including a baseball game."

Finally, the reporter asked Crush how all the people he expected would be getting home with the mainline obstructed by the train debris. "Well, that is going to be an interesting feature of the exhibition," he said. "There will be a wrecking train and crew behind each engine and the track will be cleared in a very short time. Those who have never seen wrecking trains at work on a big wreck will be entertained by this part of the program."

In talking with the *Times-Herald* man, Crush assured the reporter that his colleagues in the journalistic trade would be "looked after." Sticking with his hyperbole, he said that one thousand reporters likely would be on hand for the event and that a special stand would be built to accommodate them. Journalists would be coming from the big eastern papers as well as from Texas. He also said still photos and Kinescope (moving) images would be taken of the crash.

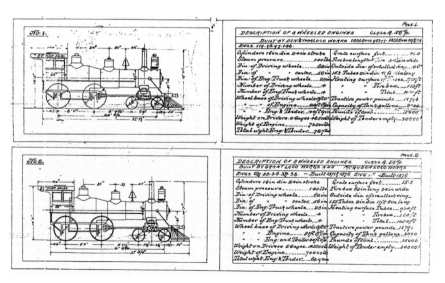

Scale drawing of one of the locomotives used in the Crush crash. *Author's collection.*

"It will be a day to be recorded in the history of Texas," Crush pronounced.

If anything could move faster than a locomotive with its throttle pushed all the way to the brass, it was shop talk. From yard to yard along the MKT system, word was spreading that the management had approved Crush's idea of smashing two locomotives together as a way to sell excursion tickets and draw attention to the Katy. Old hands, especially veteran trainmen, wondered if the passenger agent was racing wide open toward disaster—both to his career and the multiple thousands of people doubtless willing to pay to see a train wreck.

BUILDING STEAM

Crush kept it to himself if he had any doubt in his bold plan. What did preoccupy him were the hundreds of details involved in staging the spectacular event he envisioned. A prearranged crash, he was learning, had more moving parts than two steam engines.

He would have done well to consult with Alfred Streeter, and it's possible he reached out to him by mail. But after mentioning the Ohio smashup in one of his first interviews, Crush did not bring it up again. That created the perception, intentional or not, that the Texas event would be the first of its kind. Some of the news stories published during the run-up to the Texas crash made passing mention of the collision engineered by Streeter that May, but most did not.

Crush's overarching concern, of course, was getting people to buy train tickets to get to the crash site. As he had indicated before, he hoped to pull in people from all along the Katy line. To that end, the company would be offering special excursion fares to the venue from anywhere in the Katy system. Depending on location, round-trip ticket prices ranged from $2.00 to $3.50. Admission to the site itself would be free.

In one interview, Crush noted that the Katy would be spending some $20,000 on the exhibition. Being an astute businessman—and a natural-born promoter—surely the general passenger agent had put pencil to paper to come up with at least an estimate of how much he could net for his company. To reach that number, he needed paying passengers.

The main way to do that would be through advertising, both in newspapers and by plastering every stop along the Katy line with circus-like posters.

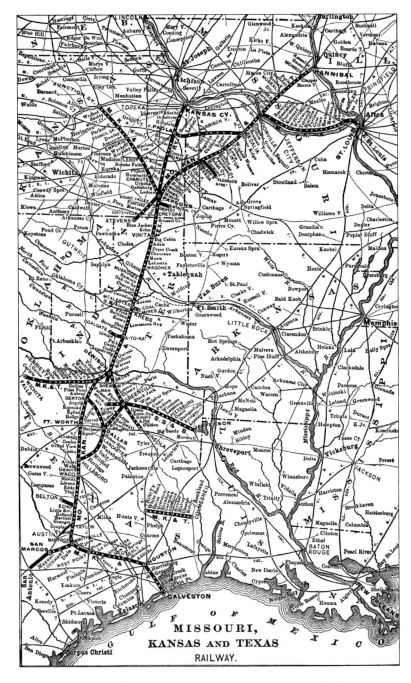

Map of Katy system showing West, Texas, the nearest depot to Crush, Texas. *Author's collection.*

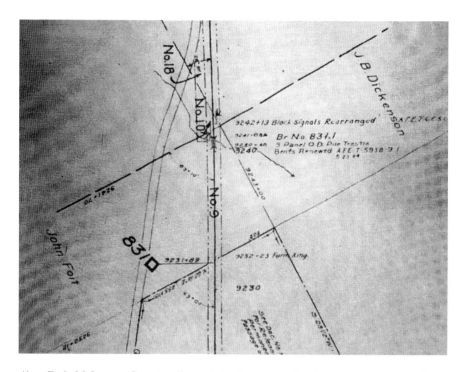

Above: Early McLennan County railroad right of way map showing acreage owned by the two farmers who leased land to the MKT for the temporary town of Crush. *McLennan County, Texas Archives.*

Opposite: Full-page newspaper advertisement showing a fanciful depiction of the coming collision at Crush. *Author's collection.*

Crush also ordered what the August 31 edition of the *Denison Sunday Gazetteer* described as "pictorial streamers advertising the contemplated head-end collision." But while the streamers ballyhooed the coming event, Crush was either deliberately playing it coy in not announcing a hard date or he was stalling so as to allow enough time for Katy workers to complete all the necessary preparation. Crush also had traveling passenger agent W.D. Lawson and local passenger agents talking up the coming crash.

As the line's general passenger agent, Crush had a lot of sway, but he still worked for a large corporation. The final decision on the date for the crash was upper management's call. On August 31, General Superintendent J.W. Maxwell and Division Superintendents A.D. Bethard and T.S. McDowell met in Dallas and, as one newspaper reported, "made a lot of figures." Indeed, "they figured over all the blank paper in all the offices." Crush must have been in the room, too, but the report did not say that.

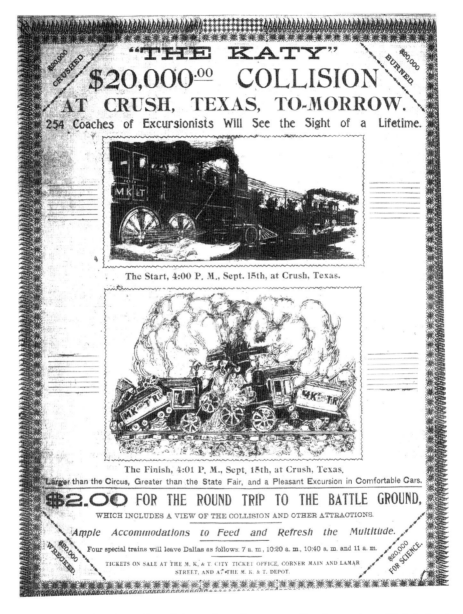

"THE KATY"
$20,000.00 COLLISION
AT CRUSH, TEXAS, TO-MORROW.
254 Coaches of Excursionists Will See the Sight of a Lifetime.

The Start, 4:00 P. M., Sept. 15th, at Crush, Texas.

The Finish, 4:01 P. M., Sept. 15th, at Crush, Texas.
Larger than the Circus, Greater than the State Fair, and a Pleasant Excursion in Comfortable Cars.
$2.00 FOR THE ROUND TRIP TO THE BATTLE GROUND,
WHICH INCLUDES A VIEW OF THE COLLISION AND OTHER ATTRACTIONS.
Ample Accommodations to Feed and Refresh the Multitude.
Four special trains will leave Dallas as follows: 7 a. m., 10:20 a. m., 10:40 a. m. and 11 a. m.
TICKETS ON SALE AT THE M. K. & T. CITY TICKET OFFICE, CORNER MAIN AND LAMAR STREET, AND AT THE M. K. & T. DEPOT.

The meeting lasted well into the afternoon. By then, the officials had nailed down the time and date for the event, worked out a schedule for all the special trains that would be running to the exhibition site and set the round-trip fares. From Fort Worth and Dallas alone, the Katy would run four special trains in addition to its regularly scheduled passenger trains. All the specials would return to their originating point immediately after the collision. For ease in determining which train, the tickets would be printed on different color stocks. Also, each train would have signage indicating its destination.

On September 2 the *Daily Monitor* of Fort Scott, Kansas, one of the towns on the Katy line, noted that Crush was making extensive preparations for the coming collision, which was planned for some time between September 15 and October 1. The story still did not say where the event would take place other than to reveal that it would be "somewhere between Hillsboro and Waco, probably at a small station, Crush, named in honor of the above-mentioned gentleman."

While the general public apparently lacked any solid details on the timing and specific location for the coming collision, the newspaper offered a figurative tip of its hat to the man behind it: "Mr. Crush is to be commended for his enterprise in this undertaking as it will be the first of its kind given west of the Mississippi."

A major variable in the planning, of course, was the crowd estimate. Since ticket sales had not yet begun, all Crush had to go on was his awareness of the number of people who had shown up for the Ohio- and Chicago-area exhibitions. Beyond that it was just a guess. "We will have at least 25,000, and probably as many as 40,000, people on the ground to witness the collision," he told a reporter following the end-of-August meeting at company headquarters. "We are making our arrangements to handle 40,000....Nobody will be discommoded."

The man in charge of making that happen was A.D. Arbegast, the Katy's bridge and building department's general foreman. He led a contingent of carpenters to the designated location along the mainline fourteen miles north of Waco. In all, some five hundred Katy employees worked fast and hard to get the venue ready for the big event, building a new town in a matter of days.

The day after their meeting at the company's main office, the Katy brass left Dallas in a special rail car for the crash site. In addition to the general superintendent and the two division superintendents, the party included Car Superintendent John Doyle, Superintendent of Motive Power J.W. Petheran, Master Mechanic C.T. McElvaney and Leo Wolfson, identified as manager of privileges. He would be overseeing food preparation and sales.

Finally, a newspaper article on September 3 confirmed that the crash would be staged "at Crush, Texas" at 4:00 p.m. on September 15. Another article noted that the instant town of Crush was near the small community of West but incorrectly said that West was in Hill County. Before he had been able to lock in that date, Crush, a lifelong Republican, had convinced what he called "the democratic clubs" to postpone the meeting they had been planning for Dallas on the fifteenth. The new date for the gathering, he told reporters, would be September 19. "You see," he said, "all the boys are going to the collision. They want to see it so strong that they are willing to postpone campaign work in order to be there." Of course, the Katy would be offering special rates to those planning on attending the rescheduled meeting.

Meanwhile, saws ripped into pine boards, hammers flew and metal clanged on metal. The railroad workers first built a 2,300-foot wooden platform along the mainline. That would be where "excursionists" would get off and on the special trains arriving from all along the Katy system. Workers also laid new track and switches adjacent to the mainline to accommodate the excursion trains, as well as company work cars and the private cars of company officials.

Under the foreman's supervision, in addition to the frame depot (where Crush had a temporary office) the railroad men also built a fifty-by-seventy-five-foot dining hall; a refreshment stand where "hop ale" would be sold; a bandstand large enough to accommodate three ensembles; three speaker's stands for politicians; two telegraph offices; a viewing stand for reporters; and a twelve-by-eighteen-foot camera stand nine feet high. The stand went up only about one hundred feet from the planned impact site.

So as to allow for a 150-foot buffer zone (one account said it was 250 feet) between the impact site and the spectators, Katy workers sunk railroad ties, drilled holes in them and then threaded cable through them to form a barrier the railroad referred to as a "dead line." Next, the carpenters would begin building thirty vendor spaces that Arbegast called "privilege stands." These, he explained to a *Denison Herald* reporter, were arranged in the "Midway Plaisance style" popularized at the Chicago World's Fair.

Judging by the Denison newspaper article (which numerous other newspapers reprinted), Arbegast would have made a fair carnival pitch man. "In these places," he said of the privilege stands, "will be located all the amusements on the ground. There will be freaks there from all over the world, and a better plaisance show has never been seen in Texas. This feature alone will be worth going to Crush to see."

In addition to the brewed hops provided by vendors, the Katy would be bringing four water cars containing eight tubs with a capacity of sixteen thousand gallons. The cars would be filled with iced artesian water from Waco. Pipes with intermittently spaced faucets would be laid from the tanks across the area where the spectators would be. Each faucet had a tin drinking cup chained to it. Katy workers also built numerous privies for the convenience of the large crowd Crush expected.

The Katy's workforce did all the building, but Crush had designed the town named in his honor. As the *Dallas Morning News* reported, "He mapped out the ground, located the lunch stands and lemonade stands, directed where the people should be placed and generally and specially is to be credited with a large share of whatever glory attaches to the success of the collision."

Nine days before the event, the September 6 edition of the *Denison Sunday Gazetteer* published a letter written on August 26 by J.M. Farnham, a former Denison resident (and possibly a former Katy employee) to a friend in Texas. Farnham said he had read about the planned collision in the August 23 edition of the paper. He wrote, "Let me say that while in Chicago last month…I witnessed one of these exciting and novel spectacles. I can assure those who attend the collision they will witness a scene that will put them to wondering how any brave engineer or fireman can ever, or has ever, come out alive from the numerous wrecks that occurred so frequently a few years ago." Farnham then went on to describe the crash Alfred Streeter had staged. Those who took in the spectacle, he concluded, "seemingly [were] well pleased for the money spent."

The same day the *Gazette* printed Farnham's letter, the *Sedalia (MO) Democrat*, rewriting a story in the *Denison Herald*, assured its readers that the coming smashup "Will Be a Sight" and "Worth Traveling Many Miles to Witness." The Missouri newspaper went on to paraphrase the Denison newspaper's praise of Crush, who it noted "has long been known as one of the most active passenger agents in the country." Calling him "a man of original ideas," the newspaper said "he has done a great deal to advertise Texas since he has been in the state and connected with the popular Katy." Still, Crush's plan to stage a "head-ender" was "drawing the attention of people in all parts of the union probably to a greater extent than anything he has heretofore undertaken." That was not hyperbole. Thanks to Crush's cozy relationship with the press, the planned Katy smashup received way more publicity than the crashes Streeter had staged earlier that year.

Waco being the nearest sizable city to the crash site, the upcoming event, as one local described it, "is the most general subject of discussion." The reporter predicted that on the day of the event, the city would be nearly depopulated "as almost everybody in Waco is arranging to attend."

While construction proceeded apace at Crush, at the Katy yard in Denison workers under the supervision of Master Mechanic C.T. McElvaney were busily preparing the two iron monsters the railroad would be sacrificing in

Steam engines used in the crash were manufactured by Grant Locomotive Works in Paterson, New Jersey. *Author's collection.*

the interest of revenue and publicity—oh yes and science. Both locomotives, Numbers 123 and 120, had been in service with the Katy since 1870. The American 4-4-0s (per the Whyte locomotive identification system, these numbers described an engine with four leading wheels on two axles followed by four larger driving wheels also on two axles and no trailing wheels), diamond-stacked, 35.5-ton engines had been completed by the Grant Locomotive Works in Paterson, New Jersey, in 1869. (One contemporary report said only one of the locomotives came from Grant, while the other from the Rogers Locomotive and Machine Works, also in Paterson, New Jersey.) Still workable if obsolete and destined for sale or the scrap heap, each locomotive would see a renewed, if short, lease on life.

The *Denison Herald* reported that the two engines were "being rebuilt, remodeled and all the latest appliances put on them, making them as good for their weight as anything the Katy has in the way of locomotives." The shop even added new seat cushions for the crews.

Not noted in the press was that McElvaney's men had stripped the locomotives of unneeded fixtures and made certain other adjustments in the interest of safety. Each of the pins in the link-and-pin couplers that would connect the cars of each train was drilled and fitted with a key that would prevent them from accidentally uncoupling. Mechanics also disabled the air pumps on the engines that fed the brake system. Doing that barred a sudden stop if an air hose broke between any of the cars. Finally, shop workers removed all tools and spare coupling pins from the engines as well as any other loose objects that might become airborne when the trains collided.

Although the MKT would not have wanted to invest any more in them than it had to, in addition to the necessary mechanical work the two engines would be getting a cosmetic makeover with ample paint and polishing. At the Denison shop, work started first on Number 123, renamed 999 for its final fling.

"When it is done it will be the handsomest, most gaudy thing in the way of a locomotive that has ever been seen on any railroad in America," the September 7 edition of the *Sedalia Democrat* rhapsodized. The tank of the engine would be painted a bright green, with yellow stripes and numbers and "an occasional touch of vermilion to add life to the effect." The boiler was being enameled black, with the wheels of the engine and tank painted vermilion, striped in blue and yellow. The cowcatcher was being painted red and green, with all the gear and trimmings of the engine and boiler "touched up with the brightest and liveliest colors." Finally, the cab would be black, green, red and blue, "showing the richest effects."

The original plan had been for the other heavyweight combatant to be prettied up at the Katy's shop in Parsons, Kansas, another division point on the line. But Denison had a larger shop, so engine Number 120, renamed 1001, was also sent to the Texas facility. It would be painted the same colors as its iron antagonist, but the scheme would be reversed. Whereas the boiler on Number 999 had been painted green, the boiler of the second engine would be painted red. One thing they would have in common was a large Katy logo on either side of their tenders. Although the old locomotives were doomed, one newspaper writer described the two refurbished pieces of rolling stock more positively. Number 1001 looked "like a bride arrayed for the wedding."

Crush, meanwhile, continued his sales spiel in the press: "I have no doubt but the new engines will be a great attraction, as public interest is at a high pitch and everybody wants to see the engines and the men who will open the throttles and leave them while running at a high rate of speed."

As soon as Katy shop workers finished with the engines, the railroad's car department began dressing up the wooden stock cars the two locomotives would be pulling. The old cars were covered with canvas to accommodate painted advertisements. Dallas's Orient Hotel, then the city's finest, paid for its name in bold letters on one of the cars. The Dallas-based State Fair of Texas also advertised itself, as did the MKT. Finally, as part of John Ringling's payoff for offering his assistance, the cars bore colorful Ringling Bros. Circus ads.

"The collision is the absorbing topic among the railroad men, and the discussion of the gold and silver question has paled into insignificance," the *Denison Herald* said. One of the things the hundreds of Katy employees were talking about was who the human participants in the locomotive duel would be. "Who will be given the honor of turning the throttles loose?" the newspaper asked in behalf of all Katy trainmen. "Who will get to build the [boiler] fires? Who will have the honor of taking charge of the trains? All these questions are asked and are as yet unanswered."

The men who made the trains go took pride in the care of the equipment they were entrusted to operate, many viewing their locomotives almost as living things with distinctive personalities. Derailments or head-on crashes were to be avoided at all cost. Considering that mindset, a natural assumption would be that Katy's trainmen would have been reluctant about being a party to Crush's scheme. Deliberately crashing an engine into another engine at high speed in front of paying spectators was a dangerous proposition, even though the crew would be leaping from the cab before impact. Jumping from a moving train was risky enough, but the forces at play in the collision itself would be tremendous. Students of physics understood that the actual amount of energy in a collision is the speed of the two bodies combined. If a boiler blew, either from too much internal pressure or from being breached, it would be like a bomb going off. Those too close to the impact who were not killed by flying metal would die from being scalded by the super-heated steam.

Despite that, Crush received scores of applications from Katy trainmen. "Old engineers want to get the speed up and jump off while the trains are going like the wind, but as yet who will have charge of them is not known," the Denison newspaper continued.

By September 10, if not before, Crush had arrived at the crash site and would remain there until the event concluded. In time to make the next edition, he wired the *Dallas Morning News* (knowing that it would share the information with its sister newspaper in Galveston) that all arrangements necessary to pull off the spectacular had been completed. The near-instant community south of West, Texas, he said, now had a population of two hundred.

"The two trains that will come together will arrive in Dallas tomorrow [September 11] and will remain [there] so that people can inspect them to their satisfaction," the *Galveston News* reported, based on Crush's telegram. "The management [of the Katy] is anxious that people shall see that they are not paper mache affairs, but first-class affairs."

While the coming event received a considerable amount of newspaper coverage, no one in the press seems to have questioned why Crush had chosen September 15 as the date for his extravaganza. That would be a Tuesday. Most adults would be at work and their children in school. Unless people chose to ask for a day off and opted to take their kids out of class, it would be hard for many folks to do the very thing Crush wanted: buy a $2.00–$3.50 excursion ticket to witness the spectacle. Weather could not have been a factor in picking the date, since long-range forecasting lay well in the future. But weather definitely would have been a concern to Crush, since September had started off wetter than average, and at that time of the year there was always the potential of tropical weather moving inland from the Gulf. (Waco, the nearest weather observation point to the crash site, would record 8.48 inches of rain that month, nearly 6 inches above average.) About all Crush could do was hope that September 15 would be rain free. By setting the time for late afternoon, Crush at least ensured that interested area residents would have time to get to the site, but the date choice surely had an impact on the size of the crowd and therefore Katy's bottom line.

Another decision made by the railroad is more easily understood. The men who would have the honor of running the two condemned locomotives were selected the way all railroads did things: by seniority. "The engineers who are to run the engines…are two old Denison boys, now running out of Smithville on the southern division," Katy conductor A.L. Dain told the *Denison Herald* a few days prior to the event. "They are Charley Cain and Charley Stanton." The other train crew members would be Frank Barnes, fireman for Number 999, and S.M. Dickenson, who would stoke the firebox of Number 1001. The conductors picked for the job were Frank Van Gilder and Thomas H. Webb.

From the large Katy yard at Smithville, the engineers deadheaded to Denison to take charge of the two old engines with a renewed, if short, lease on life. A week before the scheduled event, Cain took Number 1001 from Denison to Dallas and then Waco, stopping all along the route so that people could gawk at the soon-to-be-destroyed locomotives. With Stanton at the throttle, Number 999 went from Denison to Fort Worth and then Waco.

"It is expected that many people will throng to see it, with its holiday attire," the *Dallas Times-Herald* ventured when Number 1001 went on display

The two engineers chosen to run the doomed locomotives both worked out of MKT's Smithville, Texas division point. *Author's collection.*

at the Katy depot on September 11. "It will be almost as much interest as was the only Pompadour Jim in his holy cow days, and more than Jaggled Jim since his little argument with one Sharkey, an ex-sailor."

In invoking the slang names of the noted bare-knuckle pugilists of the day, the anonymous journalist then turned his literary imagery to one of the more decadent customs of the Roman empire, the fight-to-the-death pitting of man versus animal or man versus man in the name of mass entertainment. "A locomotive is a new departure in the way of a gladiator," he wrote. "The Romans of old enjoyed in the meeting of men and beasts, but their education was not sufficiently modern to arrange mechanical combats. That was left to a later day Roman, Crush of the Katy."

While the locomotive as gladiator metaphor was certainly apt, the venue overseen by "Crush of the Katy" fell a bit short of Rome's Flavian Amphitheater, better known as the Coliseum. But just as spectators once wagered on the success or failure of gladiators or charioteers racing at the Circus Maximus, the coming event in Central Texas would appeal to amateur and professional betting men.

--TO--

THE GREAT COLLISION

--AT--

Crush, Texas, Sept. 15.

MKT
MISSOURI, KANSAS & TEXAS RAILWAY.

Only $3.50
Round Trip.

Special train leaves Houston at 12:10 a. m., arriving at Crush 10:50 a. m., September 15. NO EXTRA CHARGE TO SEE THE COLLISION. Various forms of amusement on the grounds. Meals furnished by the Katy Dining Service Department at usual nominal rates. Many good speakers will be on hand to address the people.
For further information, call on or address
R. B. COURTNEY,
Passenger and Ticket Agent,
Houston, Texas.

Another MKT newspaper ad touting "The Great Collision." *Author's collection.*

"The gladiator locomotive will evoke as much interest as a living, breathing thing," the Dallas reporter continued, "and already there are bets being made among the railroads [*sic*] boys on which engine will stand the [day] the better. This will spread to the outside world as soon as the combatants waltz into the arena." Crush probably was too busy with the last-minute details to have had time to read of his media-made ascension to Roman citizenship, a once admired status, but likely took some ribbing about it from his colleagues.

One of those loose ends involved the distribution of posters hyping the coming crash. The Katy had commissioned an artist to produce a drawing depicting the two locomotives colliding and another showing the imagined aftermath. The two fanciful renderings were then adorned with the details of the planned collision, including the prime information as to date, location and cost of the railroad's excursion tickets. "Many people gaze at [the posters] daily and then try and dig up a couple of 53 cent silver dollars to bribe the road to let them in on the ground floor," the *Times-Herald* said.

Not everyone who saw the posters or read newspaper articles about the coming event got excited about it, at least not in the sense of being eager to see such a spectacle. Melvin Wade, an African American labor activist who had been in Dallas since Reconstruction, thought the state should intervene to derail the exhibition.

"He says the young Christian Governor and the Attorney General should be all means call an extra session of the legislature and stop the wanton destruction to property on the Katy railroad," the Dallas daily reported. "Melvin says the engines and cars which it is proposed to destroy in this wreck are worth a great deal of money to the country, and the Governor should stir himself in the interest of having plenty of engines and cars to haul the dear farmer's stuff to market."

Wade pointed out that Governor Culberson had spent "much money" in trying to prevent the Fitzsimmons-Maher fight earlier that year, but "he does not raise his hand to stop a destruction of property, and the setting of a bad example, for who knows but the Katy's jealous competitors may, in order to excel her, go to wrecking regular trains." If the governor would do nothing, Wade continued, "this wicked man Crush should be enjoined from pulling off his wreck."

That sentiment, however, constituted a decidedly minority opinion. The coming Crash at Crush was the primary topic of conversation in Dallas and elsewhere in the state and along the Katy line, for the time being putting the figurative air brakes to political discourse and other matters.

Before heading to Dallas with Number 1001, engineer Cain had demonstrated that in addition to his seniority on the line, he possessed a sense of humor. Arriving in North Texas on September 9, he soon wrote a letter to Crush:

> *Dear Sir: Inasmuch as I am one of the engineers to handle an engine at the great prearranged collision at the town named in your honor, I beg to submit you the following:*
>
> *The vocation of a locomotive engineer is an honorable and high calling. More than usual honor is added to the calling by the fact that I have been selected as one of the engine men to get the rains [sic] together under a full head of steam; therefore, I humbly ask that you provide a safe, sure and speedy pony, equipped and ready at the point where I am to leave the engine so that I may mount and ride into the scene in due form becoming and befitting the dignity of an engineer, for you yourself can readily see how undignified it would appear for me to go plodding along like a plebian to the wreck after all is over.*
>
> *I submit this to your consideration, hoping that you will see the dignity and gravity of the situation and save me a long walk.*
>
> *Very respectfully,*
> *Charles Cain*

At 11:10 a.m. on Sunday, September 13, the southbound Katy, pulling more than the normal number of passenger cars and one company car for MKT officials, hissed to a stop at the exhibition site. Among the many passengers alighting from the train was a reporter with the *Dallas Morning News*.

Sticking to the conventional third-person voice used by journalists of the day, he wrote, "When a reporter for The News stepped from the platform… the first thing he saw was a great big sign reading, 'Crush Station.' The next thing he saw was General Superintendent J.W. Maxwell, who was busy with his [train] operators and stenographers." He didn't mention, but could not have missed, another freshly painted sign along the tracks that read "Point of Collision."

The unnamed journalist was pleased to see that two telegraph offices had been opened at the new station, one on either end of the long siding the railroad had built. Realizing that the train dispatcher would keep one of the wires tied up once the event ended, he hoped he wouldn't have trouble getting his dispatches back to his newspaper's city room.

Given the time of his arrival, likely the *Morning News* staffer's next stop was the Katy's large meal service facility, located "away up on top of the hill" from the newly built depot. Doubtless enjoying his lunch that day courtesy the Katy, the reporter noted that "the food has been specially prepared for Mr. [F.E.] Miller [the railroad's St. Louis–based food service manager] by the best known packers in America and everything will be served in the best of style. None of the privilege men [other vendors] will be allowed to sell lunch." Nor would any alcohol be sold on the grounds, "this being a local option precinct." The reporter said Katy officials had selected the site for that reason, but they hadn't. And he was wrong about no alcohol being sold.

Later that day, both of the "contestants" in the coming metal-on-metal locomotive duel did a trial run. Thanks to Crush, the *Morning News* reporter got to ride on Number 1001, the locomotive run by engineer Cain. Also along for the ride were Master Mechanic McElvaney, Traveling Engineer A.C. Loucks and Crush.

"The run was just a mile and stop watches were held so that no mistake could be made," the Dallas reporter wrote. "The engine was…heated up well, and with the steam gauge showing 135 pounds [per square inch] the start was made. She moved off very slowly, but in two seconds was rushing along, and in half a minute was going like the wind, and all the boys had to hold on hard to keep from being shaken off. When the watches were consulted the hands showed that the mile had been made in one minute and a fraction of a second, or an average speed of more than 58 miles an hour."

Stanton ran his Number 999 next, making the mile in about the same time. Each engineer would make three practice runs, since it was critical for both safety and the benefit of the photographers that the two trains meet exactly where they were supposed to. That meant their speed had to

One of the few surviving MKT excursion tickets. This one provided passage from Dallas to Crush, Texas, and back. *Author's collection.*

be consistent. "On each engine," Number 999 fireman Frank Barnes later revealed, "a clamp was placed, against which the throttle could be opened. In this way, the same throttle setting could be used each time."

The day before the event, the *Houston Post* and other dailies along the Katy system ran a display ad touting the "crush at Crush." The special excursion train would be leaving the Bayou City's MKT Depot at 12:10 a.m. Tuesday and arrive at Crush at 4:00 p.m. just in time for the show. "Do not miss this opportunity to see the only prearranged collision which has ever been given west of the Mississippi," the ad cautioned. Round-trip fare would be $3.50.

Katy's competitors would also be cashing in on the big event. The International and Great Northern Railroad, for example, ran an ad touting a two-dollar special round-trip rate to Crush for that day. So did the Santa Fe and other railroads.

Starting on Monday, September 14, thousands of people clutching round-trip excursion tickets began boarding Katy trains all along the MKT system bound for a town that had grown in a cornfield practically overnight. "Everything in the shape of a good engine and all rolling stock on the Katy is being pressed into service for the occasion," the *Dallas Morning News* reported in a dispatch from Denison. "The yards here this afternoon were as great a sight as Chicago ever saw, with thirty fully equipped passenger trains pulling out in all directions in which the road has a line out of the city."

"THE MOST NOVEL EXPERIMENT EVER GIVEN IN TEXAS"

When the sun rose that late summer morning, it exposed a clear, pale blue sky. It would be a hot, sultry day, but otherwise Mother Nature had done her part for the Katy. Rain did not seem at all likely.

Now everything was up to general passenger agent Crush. While he was not the ranking MKT official on hand, he had operational control of the event. As such, even though he had high confidence that everything would go as planned, he knew his job could be on the line if anything went wrong.

Already, Katy excursion trains were stacking up at the Crush depot, disgorging excited passengers by the hundreds. Dozens more trains were on the way, including three excursion trains coming from Denison. Riding on one of those specials was MKT trainman M.J. Heaney, who had been assigned to accompany conductor Frank Butts to the temporary town.

"There were about twelve cars with passengers riding the platforms and standing up in the aisles," Heaney recalled. "We left about midnight. About half of the crowd was drunk, and after passing Fort Worth, the air was pulled on us quite frequently [referring to train's emergency brakes, then located in the washroom of each coach]….We had quite a time searching the cars and washrooms for some of the drunks who were continually pulling the rope of the air valve."

After reaching the Crush depot and discharging all the passengers, including many a fellow with a budding hangover that could only be made bearable by food or a little "hair of the dog," the engineer backed the train to Hillsboro, where it would remain until he received orders to return to the crash venue. At the Katy's busy Hillsboro depot, Heaney caught the next excursion train back to Crush. On that train, he ran into his friend Alex Atchison, Katy's chief engineer. After getting off the train, the two men looked around for a good vantage point, preferably one with shade. "Atchison and I found shelter from the sun under one of the few trees in the neighborhood," he continued. "Our tree was very near the track and my friend suggested we find a more distant place to view the wreck." That proved to have been a very good idea.

As had Heaney and Atchison, most Katy employees who could get time off were at Crush for the event. Scores of Katy workers who were on the clock were on hand to handle a variety of duties ranging from dispatching trains to and from the crash venue to food preparation. Other workmen had nothing to do until it came time to clear the tracks of wreckage after the collision.

Off-duty freight conductor Charlie (Kid) Hurdleson, after examining the opposing trains, let it be known that he would bet fifty dollars that he could ride the last car behind one of the locomotives and not be hurt in the crash. He wagered another fifty dollars that the car wouldn't even leave the track. "Trainmaster [Albert D.] Bethard got wind of Hurdleson's wager and threatened to discharge him if he made the attempt," Heaney recalled. Hurdleson stayed off the train and kept his job.

A reporter with the afternoon *Dallas Times-Herald* had been at the event site since 7:00 a.m. Although most of the spectators had traveled to Crush on Katy excursion trains, he noted that several thousand local residents had come by "private conveyance," and more were arriving by the minute. Already, the hillsides on either side of the Katy tracks "were fairly alive with people, horses, buggies, wagons, carts, etc." The area to the west of the tracks was where the "excursionists" were congregated. Most of the people on the east side of the tracks were locals.

Eighteen-year-old Horace Creswell had a job in the small McLennan County town of Mount Calm, but the young Memphis, Tennessee native wasn't about to miss the big doings in Crush that afternoon. He took a Cotton Belt Line train to Waco, where he intended to board one of the Katy excursion trains. "There were thousands of people on the train," he later recalled. "I couldn't get inside, so I climbed on top with some other young fellows. We made the 14 miles out there alright."

The Belton correspondent for the *Temple Times* left the depot at the Bell County seat aboard one of the Katy special trains at 10:00 a.m., arriving at the event site between noon and 1:00 p.m. "There were a number of entertainments on the ground and lunch stands, etc.," he wrote. "We could not get beer, but if we were to call for malt tonic, we could get anything we wanted. We put in the time the best we could for four or five hours looking at the engines that so soon were to be engaged in mortal combat."

Here's how another visitor described the carnival-like scene: "Fakirs of all classes were there; there were snake-charmers and side-shows, flying jennies [merry go rounds] and freaks of nature, and as one passed along the eye became dizzy and blinded with an ever varying succession of showy business enterprises."

In addition to drinking, eating and taking in all the side show entertainment, attendees listened to an assortment of political candidates espouse their positions. And still the crowd continued to grow. The *Dallas Times-Herald* journalist said the throng represented "every trade, profession and vocation in life, from the humblest plow-boy to the highest-toned politician and lawyer." Nor was the "fair sex" under represented, he added.

In all, the Katy would roll at least thirty-three excursion trains (an article published only a year after the event said the final count had been forty-seven trains) totaling more than 250 cars to Crush. For hours, a new train arrived every five to ten minutes. As soon as they unloaded, most of the northbound trains backed down to Waco, while the majority of the southbound trains rolled in reverse up the line to Hillsboro to await telegraphic orders from the MKT dispatcher posted at Crush to return at the end of the event to carry everyone back home. The Katy had laid track adjacent to its mainline to accommodate the special trains, but that was not sufficient to handle all the rolling stock that converged on Crush.

By 10:00 a.m., an estimated ten thousand people milled around at Crush, with more spectators continuing to pour in by train and wagon and on foot. Working in the dining hall the Katy had built, the railroad's top food man had eight employees helping him prepare and sell sandwiches, frankfurters, sauerkraut and pies, but he had to put in a frantic request for more people. More frugal folks, mostly the locals, had shown up with picnic baskets. As the temperature rose, so did the consumption of the free water and the for-purchase lemonade and beer. On the midway, people took in the sights, and while generally having a good time, they had to watch their wallets. Pickpockets were about, and one scam artist was selling realistic-looking cigars that turned out to be made of wood.

As the scheduled time of the crash approached, the small town of Crush, only a few weeks old, had mushroomed into one of the state's largest cities, maybe the largest. No one ever knew the exact number of people

This image, not published since December 1896, shows the crowd at Crush before the two about-to-be-sacrificed locomotives arrived. It is believed to have been based on a photo taken by Jervis Deane that has since been lost. *Author's collection.*

who showed up, but newspaper estimates ranged from fifteen thousand on the low side to thirty to fifty thousand. One account said it was the biggest crowd to that point in Texas history, excluding the previous year's Tennessee Day at the state fair in Dallas. If more than forty thousand people were there, and most accounts say there were, Crush was indeed the largest city in the state that day.

"Men, women and children, lawyers, doctors, merchants, farmers, artisans, clerks representing every class and grade of society were scattered around over the hillsides or clustered around the lunch stands, discussing with eager anticipation the exciting event they had come so far to see," the *Galveston News* reported.

A young man named James Casey borrowed a saddle and a bridle and rode his best bay pony from the small farming community of Axtell to the "collision grounds," as he later referred to the event site. "I tied my pony to the fence on the public road and by a heroic effort procured a reserved seat in the top of an elm sapling. It was one of the best positions on the grounds for safety and observation."

Among those arriving for the big show were brothers Jervis Corydon, Martin O. and Granville M. Deane. Waco photographer Jervis Deane had been commissioned by the Katy to be the event's official photographer, and he, in turn, had asked Martin and Granville to assist him. Martin had come down from Fort Worth, where he had a studio, and Granville had traveled south from Dallas, where he did business. Now they busied themselves setting up their tripod-mounted cameras on the photography platform while New Yorker Enoch Rector did last-minute checks of his state-of-the-art motion picture camera.

In all the hype leading up to the event, Crush had said he expected one thousand reporters would come to witness the crash. Many of the state's dailies and country weeklies did have credentialed staff members present that day—their transportation comped by the Katy or covered by an advertising swap—but more likely there were several dozen journalists there to cover the collision, not hundreds.

From the vantage point of their platform, the badge-wearing reporters looked down on what a scribe for the *San Antonio Express* called "a perfect sea of humanity," a veritable ocean represented by thousands of bobbing straw hats, caps, derbies and black Stetsons. Despite the heat, a fair number of the men wore suit coats or black vests, but most had on only long-sleeved, high-collared white shirts X-ed in the back by the suspenders holding up their trousers. The ladies, cooling themselves with hand fans or standing under parasols, had turned out in their finery—narrow-waist, puff-sleeved blouses and long skirts. Big hats abloom with faux flowers and real feathers topped their heads.

Crush, whom the Galveston newspaper described as "the grand marshal of the occasion," had chosen to manage the event from the saddle of a tall, spirited white horse. Wearing a white pith helmet and a blue sash (one account said it was red) across his chest, he herded women and children toward the shade afforded by a line of trees along a ravine west of the crash site. Thoughtfully, he had ordered seats set up there. Nearby ran a creek where locals watered their horses and mules. The men had to stand in the sun and swelter.

Two hundred special deputies under the command of the McLennan County sheriff (some newspaper accounts said there were only one hundred temporary lawmen) had been sworn in at nearby West earlier that day to provide police protection and crowd control. Wearing red badges, the men were paid by the railroad. Despite the size of the crowd, other than trying to keep people a safe distance from what the press called "the deadline," the officers only made eight criminal cases, all misdemeanors. One of those arrests was an African American boy who threw a rock at a white youth.

"He was promptly arrested and placed in the calaboose," the *Sherman Herald* reported. "In making the arrest one of the officers fired his gun in the air. This gave rise to all sorts of rumors."

Other rowdies may have been placed in the MKT-built temporary jail to cool down or sober up only to be released later without any charges filed against them. Contemporary reports did say that a fair number of attendees had consumed too much alcohol.

No matter the rich Czech heritage of beer drinking, Crush lay in a dry precinct. While officially only free ice water from the Katy and lemonade sold by vendors, other tents offered "hop ale" (beer) and "so forth" (whiskey). One attendee later recalled that around the various vendors corks extracted from beer bottles rose knee-high before the end. Plenty of spectators also brought their own bottles.

Just a barefoot boy, Kemp Plunkett rode in a wagon with his father to Crush from their residence on the east side of Waco. "Mother packed sandwiches for our noonday lunch," he recalled, "but forgot to put in drinking water. As we waited in a cotton patch, I got mighty thirsty. I saw other people drinking from various type[s] of bottles, but Dad said they weren't drinking water and I couldn't have any."

Thanks to West livery stable co-owner J.M. Smith, none of the many horses and mules at the crash site would go hungry either. Happy to cash in on all the traffic, Smith set up at Crush to sell shelled oats, corn and bundles of fodder to anyone needing feed for their animals. He sold out well before the crash.

The size of the crowd delighted Crush, but he and the special officers were having trouble keeping people behind the boundary set up to prevent spectators from getting too close to the tracks. "Mr. Crush was doing his best to keep the crowd back," photographer Jervis Deane's wife, Maude, recalled. "He was riding about on his horse overlooking everything and doing the best he could for the safety of the people." She said Crush even asked her to leave the photography platform, and she complied.

Dr. O.L. Williams of Dallas, who traveled to Crush with his wife and another couple, was standing with his party just west of the photographer's platform wondering when the show would start when William Crush rode up. "[He] stated that the cause of the delay of the collision was his inability to clear the ground between the cables…and that he was afraid to risk it until the ground was clear." From where Williams and the others were standing, Crush rode to the photographer's stand and "shouted [to the spectators inside the danger zone] at the top of his voice…'to get back, for every one of them were in danger of losing their lives.'" Williams would remember that Crush's "emphatic and earnest warning caused the crowd to sway backwards toward the cable."

The only crowd-control measure that worked for Crush was resorting to what the *Galveston News* called "the positive threat" that the crash would be canceled if the eager spectators did not move farther back from the track. "The great crowd was difficult to manage and much time was lost forcing people to retire," the *San Antonio Express* reported. "A wonderful recklessness marked the conduct of many."

The man in charge that afternoon would have questioned the use of the word *wonderful* to describe the crowd's demeanor. Clearly, most of them wanted to have as good a view as possible, and few seemed concerned about being too close to the coming collision. "I begged, entreated, threatened and commanded them to seek places of safety," Crush later told the *Dallas Morning News*. "They paid no more attention to me or the 200 constables than if we had nothing to do with the affair."

As Crush continued his efforts, after the final excursion train emptied and departed, railroad workers pulled up a section of track behind each of the opposing trains. That would preclude the disastrous scenario of one train derailing and the other running wild and crew-less on the Katy's mainline. The Katy's mainline was then closed to through traffic.

"At 3 o'clock in the afternoon one of the collision trains steamed slowly over the course and was greeted with a loud cheer," the *Galveston News* said. "Then the other came down from its berth on a side track and was also loudly cheered."

The crash had been set for 4:00 p.m., but to give him more time to corral the crowd, Crush pushed the time back an hour. At 5:00 p.m., at his order, the two trains approached each other again for a final nose-to-nose mechanical salute. After Marvin Deane had exposed a glass negative of the final, nonviolent meeting of the two locomotives, one of the trains backed up the hill to the south while the other backed uphill to the north.

Back in place, Number 1001 waited at milepost 832 to the north of the planned impact point, while Number 999 sat to the south at milepost 830. With each train one mile away from the planned crash site, neither engine could be seen by the spectators. The crowd waited "with bated breath," as did the train crews. "Time crawled by and still the signal [to roll] did not come," Barnes remembered.

Crush and other Katy officials "were grouped about the little telegraph office not fifty feet from the place of contact, with watches in hand, waiting for the whistle which would tell them that the trains were ready to start on the fatal journey." Then came two long whistle blasts.

"Everything was now ready," the *Galveston News* continued. "The smoke was pouring from their funnels in a great black streak and the popping of the steam could be distinctly heard for the distance of a mile. People were standing on tip-toe from every point of vantage trying to see every movement of the wheels that were so soon to roll to destruction."

The railroad had strung telegraph wire from the Crush depot to the two staging points where the opposing green and red locomotives sat with steam up. A telegrapher at each end would notify the engineer as soon as he got the word from Crush for them to start.

"Finally," Barnes continued, "late in the afternoon, our operator hollered 'Two minutes!' and raised his hand." When that interim had passed, Crush waved his sunhat, the crowd cheered and the depot telegrapher tapped out three dashes and a dot, "G," followed by three dashes, "O." It was 5:10 p.m.

"The rumble of the two trains, faint and far off at first, but growing nearer and more distinct with each fleeting second, was like the gathering of a cyclone," the *Galveston News* said. "Nearer and nearer they came, the whistles of each blowing repeatedly, and the [signal] torpedoes [small metal pillows of explosive with straps attached] which had been placed on the track exploding in almost a continuous round like the rattle of musketry. Every eye was trained and every nerve on edge."

The Galveston newspaper went on to describe the vantage point the paying spectators had:

> For 100 feet to the west of the track there is a level plain and then you strike a branch of the dry bed of a creek. The banks of this creek rise almost perpendicularly and it is on these banks that the crowd was stationed. They had a commanding view of everything that happened. They could see both trains when they started and every revolution of the wheels…the dark lines of the cars limned out against the darker forms of the trees beyond. [To the east] they could see away off in the green and level plain in front of them, the farmers in the doors with their wives and children about them, watching the most wonderful thing that ever happened in that part of the world.

Engineer Cain, following the exacting protocol that had been developed, opened the throttle to the preset clamp, counted sixteen puffs of steam (which would have been four revolutions of the driver), moved the reverse lever to the second notch and then leaped from his glory-bound locomotive.

Shaking Hands.

Views of the Head End Collision at Crush, Texas, September 15, 1896.

Photographed by *Deane* Of DALLAS, Fort Worth, Waco and Houston.

The doomed Katy locomotives "shaking hands" prior to their high-speed crash. *Baylor University Texas Collection.*

Picking up speed, the two locomotives—their whistles rigged to blast with each rotation of the driver wheels—raced toward each other. The trains now only a quarter-mile apart, sudden panic hit Crush in his gut. The train crews were supposed to jump off after their locomotives traveled thirty yards. But Crush saw only five trainmen bail out, three from Number 1001 and only two from the other engine. What had happened to the sixth man? To his horror, he thought that one of the men must have decided to stay with the train—a foolish, unauthorized move that meant the man's certain death.

What Crush didn't know was that one of the engineers had decided to put on a little show of his own and wait until the last thirty seconds before leaping. "I later learned that Charlie Stanton had arranged with a section crew to plant a pile of cinders, a quarter of a mile from where the trains were scheduled to meet," Crush recalled. "He landed on the cinders, safe and sound." If any of the men who jumped from either train got skinned up or bruised, it was never mentioned.

Counting the seconds that passed before the locomotives reached full speed, each traveling downhill on a 2 percent grade (an elevation drop of 105.6 feet), it took only two minutes for the engines to close the distance between them. When the trains became visible to the crowd, as the *Times-Herald* reported, some people put their hands over their ears, closed their eyes and turned their backs to the tracks. Mothers gathered in their children. But most of the spectators stood their ground, determined to get their $2.00 to $3.50 worth. One woman remarked that the engines were too pretty to destroy.

"Now they were within ten feet of each other, the bright red and green paint on the engines and the gaudy advertisements on the cars showing clear and distinct in the glaring sun," the Galveston newspaper continued. At that moment, one of the photographers whose job it was to document the crash tripped the shutter of his camera. The image captured the trains as they were virtually head-to-head, seconds from impact.

"Each one [in the crowd] seemed to be holding his breath...and then words fail to describe the scene," the writer from Belton later reported. That said, the unnamed journalist gave it a try anyway: "Imagine two monstrous pieces of mechanism coming together as fast as the greatest power in the world could give them."

"A SCENE THAT WILL HAUNT A MAN"

The crew of Number 999, reunited with their showboat engineer, watched their train speeding downhill toward its destruction. "[W]e saw a great cloud of steam and saw parts of the engine flying through the air," fireman Frank Barnes recalled. "From that sickening sight and from the roar of the sound, we knew that the unexpected had happened—a boiler explosion. We watched numbly, praying that nobody had been killed or hurt."

Since no one remained on either locomotive to read the instruments, the exact speed of the two trains at impact is not known. If the planned-for 60 miles an hour had been reached, the energy released at impact was equivalent to a 120-mile-per-hour collision. Factoring in the huge mass of the locomotives and the six box cars each pulled, the forces at play were devastatingly destructive. But even more powerful energy was about to be released.

The two engines struck, rose up to briefly form an upside-down "V" and then, like two fighting mustangs, began tearing each other apart. The first three box cars pulled by northbound Number 999 telescoped into one another, while four of the box cars behind Number 1001 disintegrated on impact. And then catastrophe.

"A crash, sound of timbers rent and torn, and then a shower of splinters," the *Galveston News* correspondent wrote. "There was just a swift instant of silence, and then, as if controlled by a single impulse, both boilers exploded simultaneously and the air was filled with flying missiles of iron and steel varying in size from a postage stamp to half a driving

The Trains Just as They Struck.

Views of the Head End Collision at Crush, Texas, September 15, 1896.

Photographed by *Deane,*

OF DALLAS,
FORT WORTH,
Waco and Houston

The two locomotives racing toward each other only seconds before impact. *Baylor University Texas Collection.*

wheel, falling indiscriminately on the just and unjust, the rich and poor, the great and small."

Young Creswell, who had ridden on top of one of the excursion trains bound for Crush, suddenly realized that he had been standing way too close to the tracks. "There was a big cloud of steam and bolts…and bolts and things like that flying through the air," he recalled. "I was about 30 feet from the place where the trains hit, but nothing hit me. The top off one of the locomotives sailed right over my head, it looked like a big buzzard." He said the trains met only roughly ten feet from the "Point of Collision" sign.

James Casey, who traveled twelve miles on horseback from Axtell to see the crash, later reasoned that "every one stood a chance to get killed that was in a half mile of the collision" but that he didn't believe "many thought of grim death stalking around among that multitude of joyful people" before the crash.

The last thing photographer Jervis Deane saw before a flying bolt slammed into his right eye. *Baylor University Texas Collection.*

Another man in the crowd, seeing two big hunks of hot metal coming his way, started running as fast as he could. Suddenly, he tripped and fell flat on the ground. One of the missiles flew past him, while the other came down just next to him, embedding itself vertically into the soil like a giant fallen meat cleaver. When the shaky spectator got to his feet, he realized that the metal had sliced off his coattails.

Maude Deane, wife of photographer Jervis Deane, described the collision's unexpected aftermath: "When the explosion occurred it was like what I have read of battles. Projectiles were flying in every direction and it seems to me something of a miracle that so few people were struck. I saw a ponderous fragment barely miss a little boy."

A.K. Ragsdale, who had come with a friend from Palestine in East Texas, sought shelter under a cold drink stand when the iron hailstorm started. Unfortunately, he and his buddy weren't the only ones who had that idea.

"The crowd wrecked the stand trying to get under it," he recalled. "So all we could do was dodge. I well remember the jacket of one of the engines, which flew by, big as an elephant."

Several shudder-inducing seconds of silence followed the boiler explosions as the onlookers tried to comprehend what had just happened. Then, as the *Dallas Times-Herald* described it, "the crowd with one united cheer rushed pell-mell to the scene of the wreck, breaking down the ropes used for dead lines, climbing over bushes and in many instances running over those who were slow or had stumbled."

Within minutes, a swarm of spectators scrambling to collect souvenirs covered the "mass of ruin." Others climbed up on the surviving box cars for a better view of the wreckage. While the *Times-Herald* reporter said he had not been able to determine who scooped up the first piece of one or the other locomotives, he could report that Dallas resident J.M. Work was seen emerging from the crowd with a piece of wood in his hand and shouting that he had succeeded in picking up the second piece.

Fanciful depiction of the crash executed circa 1960 by Robert R. Abernathy, a Waco photographer and commercial artist. The large-scale piece, of which this is only a portion, hangs in the Texas Collection at Baylor University in Waco. *Photo by Mike Cox.*

Katy trainman Heaney, like so many others, was just thankful to be alive. "The crown sheet of one of the engines [shot] up in the air like a dove and dropped about a quarter of a mile from the wreck," he said. "It was a very good thing that we had moved away from the tree…as some of the iron from the locomotive blew into the tree, injuring some of the spectators roosting there."

Other spectators had not been so lucky. People lay dead or dying, and more had been wounded. Many others, still standing, had sustained abrasions or contusions or burned their hands picking up pieces of metal they hadn't realized were hot. Screams of pain and cries of grief were nearly drowned out by the din of the crowd.

"The crowd seemed to be indifferent as to the catastrophe," Maude Deane told a reporter. "They were rushing about picking up fragments eagerly and only a few gave attention to the wounded. Each one of the sufferers had his own party around him, but the general disposition was to collect souvenirs."

Despite the size of the throng, only a handful of written accounts by non-journalist witnesses are known to exist. One description of the events at Crush came from schoolteacher Maggie Dunn of Axtell, a small town in eastern McLennan County. She included her account in a letter she wrote the following day to her sweetheart and future husband, Will Clift of Pottsboro.

These are the 259 words she devoted to the crash:

> Well, I really did go to Crush. Florence and I went together…didn't decide to go until about fifteen minutes before train time.
>
> We had a great time too—stayed in Waco until after twelve and then went out to Crush. Met up with Mr. Rounsaville—Florence's sweetheart—at the Katy depot. He was with us then the rest of the day—don't know how we would have managed without him, he was so nice to us.
>
> I won't attempt to describe the collision only 'twas just "awful"; and they certainly did "crush." We couldn't see anything of the engines—nothing but smoke.
>
> I never saw such a pell-mell rush just after the two engines struck—we ran just as hard as anybody. We managed to get in two or three feet of the wreck, but were forced to turn back. It was just like being in a hot furnace—had to fan all the time to keep from suffocating. It was all we could do to keep from being trampled upon, but we managed to escape.
>
> One or two timbers fell in about twenty feet of where we stood, but feel very thankful that we were not hurt.

> *I say five that were wounded, four of them dangerously. The young lady that was killed lived only five miles from here.*
>
> *How every grateful the rest of us should feel that we were not at all injured—I had no idea there was any danger, but I wouldn't have thought of getting so near it as a great many did.*

While unhurt, the young woman did suffer some adversity: she lost her billfold on the train back to Waco. Otherwise her return trip went smoothly, which was not the norm that evening.

"Owing to some unexplained hitch," the *Denison Sunday Gazette* reported five days later, "it was two hours before the first train pulled out with the living freight, and it was 9 o'clock or after before the last train got away, and then there was a delay of nearly two hours at Hillsboro. The train did not arrive at Denison until 7:30 the next morning."

Actually, according to the reporter covering the crash for the *Austin Statesman*, the aftermath was far worse than the pro-Katy Denison paper made it seem. Following the crash, the *Statesman* said, "a wild race to get away began." But no trains showed up until about 6:30 p.m. By that time, as the Denison newspaper reported, "the crowds were packed along each side of the track for two miles, making it almost impossible for the [train] cars to pass through. The first train left the grounds at 7 o'clock, and from that time until nearly 11 o'clock the crowds packed and jammed each other, men and women alike fighting for places on departing trains."

Near chaos prevailed. "No one knew which train to take, and train officials seemed unable to give them any intelligence," the capital city journalist continued. "Thousands were hauled into Waco and dumped, and for several hours sought in vain some information as to how to get away, and many finally gave up in despair and went to hotels for the night. The crowd was immense, the confusion most pronounced, and the result was [a] tired, home-sick and hungry crowd. Many had not tasted food since early morning, as the lunch stands at the grounds soon gave out."

Some two thousand people from Waco had traveled to Crush for the crash. When word reached the city that the collision "had resulted in a fatal catastrophe a thrill of horror ran through hundreds of people." The MKT Depot, the telegraph office, police headquarters and the Sheriff's Office were overrun with worried parents, siblings and spouses wanting to know who had been killed and injured. "Excitement continued great on the streets until a late hour," the *Galveston News* said the next morning.

The Austin journalist further noted that the departing spectators he saw were "weary and weather-washed," crowded into passenger cars "packed to suffocation." He concluded, "While [the] holiday wrecking was great, it was hardly greater than the mass of humanity who presented a totally wrecked appearance…as they stood in the moonlight alongside of the track and impatiently waited an opportunity to catch a train for anywhere."

Describing the outcome of the crash two days later, the September 17 edition of the *Dallas Morning News* spoke for most of those who had been in Crush: "It [was] a scene that will haunt a man…make him nervous whenever he hears an engine whistle, and disturb his dreams with black clouds of death-dealing iron hail, but it is not to be set down on paper."

PICKING UP THE PIECES

As soon as the deadly shrapnel fall ended, reporters climbed down from the observation deck and sprinted to one or the other of the two on-site telegraph shacks to wire their respective editors that the Katy crash had not gone as planned. Details would follow as they became available.

Katy personnel and doctors on the scene got the more seriously wounded on the first train to Waco. From the MKT Depot there, the victims were rushed by horse-drawn conveyance to Waco's largest and finest accommodation, the Pacific Hotel, for treatment by local physicians, including MKT contract surgeon Dr. Garland B. Foscue. Hospitals were not common then, and Waco did not yet have one. The less seriously injured were left to fend for themselves or to be helped by friends or family.

How the unexpected boiler explosions affected the man who had planned the spectacle can only be surmised, but Crush had no time for reflection. He had left on the first train to arrange for the care of the injured spectators. "Mr. Crush is now in Waco, giving his personal attention to the matter, and will remain there as long as his services are necessary," his chief clerk, Randolph Daniels, told a reporter the next day.

Crush's rapid departure may have been inspired by more than his concern for the injured spectators. Crash witness A.K. Ragsdale, who would go on to a long career with the Cotton Belt Railroad, remembered years later that once the stunned spectators began to realize that the collision had resulted in deaths and injuries, sentiment arose to lynch Crush. None of the contemporary newspaper accounts of the crash and its aftermath mentions

Before the Crowd Got to the Wreck.
Views of the Head End Collision at Crush, Texas, September 15, 1896.
Photographed by *Deane*, Of DALLAS, Fort Worth, Waco and Houston,

Moments after the twin boiler explosions, stunned spectators began moving toward the wreckage. *Baylor University, Texas Collection.*

talk of a proposed necktie party for the Katy's general passenger agent, but extrajudicial hangings were certainly not unknown in Texas back then.

Arriving in Waco, Crush saw to it that Dr. Foscue attended to the injured. Crush would have stayed in Waco longer, but waiting for him at the Katy depot was a telegram from the line's corporate office in St. Louis ordering him to report there "at once." He spent a restless night at the Pacific Hotel and left early the next morning on the first northbound passenger train. He figured his career with the Katy was over, no less ruined than the two trains he had wrecked.

Most of the reporters who saw the crash wired a story to their respective newspapers and then boarded one of the special trains for home. But some—including representatives of the Austin, Dallas and Galveston newspapers—spent the night in Waco and returned to the scene the next day to gather information for follow-up stories.

One of those journalists was the correspondent for the *Austin Statesman*. He filed a second-day story reporting that all was quiet at Crush on the day after the event where thousands had gathered "to witness one of the most thrilling scenes ever enacted in Texas."

The Crowd at the Wreck.

Views of the Head End Collision at Crush, Texas, September 15, 1896.

Photographed by *Deane.* Of DALLAS, Fort Worth, Waco and Houston.

Spectators swarming around the crash site collecting souvenirs. *Baylor University, Texas Collection.*

Almost immediately after the crash, Katy track men had replaced the rails they had pulled up prior to the collision and then started working on a "shoo fly," temporary trackage that would allow traffic to continue along the mainline until the wreckage could be cleared. That job was undertaken by two wrecker trains, each with a steam-powered crane capable of lifting twenty tons. With one crane working at each end of the debris, by 8:30 p.m. the tracks had been cleared. The fast Katy Flyer, which ran from St. Louis to Galveston in thirty-seven hours, had been delayed for twenty-five minutes, "but," as the *Statesman* staffer reported "the wrecking crew did such efficient work that everything is in apple pie order this morning."

In addition to clearing the tracks as quickly as possible, Katy workers loaded the larger pieces of debris—long portions of the two locomotive's boilers, wheels, axles, side rods and other train parts—on flatcars for eventual

The Crash at Crush delayed the premier Katy Flyer passenger train by only twenty-five minutes. *Author's collection.*

salvage as scrap iron. Since the Crush depot was only three miles south of the depot at West, the railroad had no use for it after the crash. Workers tore down all the frame structures erected for the event and offered the lumber to the property owners. John Foit used the wood he got to build a new barn on his nearby farm. Whether the railroad gathered up the smaller pieces of debris not collected by souvenir hunts was not reported. Someone with the Katy also offered Foit the brass bell from one of the locomotives, but the practical-minded farmer said he had no use for it and declined the gift.

A.J. Harralson, chief clerk with Katy's bridge and building department, found a portion of a boiler that had been blown four hundred feet from the tracks. "The piece of steel was 12 feet long and four feet wide at its widest point," he told a reporter with the *Sherman Herald*. "Fortunately it fell away from the group of spectators." Another Katy employee said he had seen one of the boiler flues that had landed near a house a half mile west of the collision point.

As the wrecking crew worked to move what remained of Number 1001, one of the men found an open-faced Hamilton railroad pocket watch in the debris. Undamaged and still ticking, the tough timepiece was returned to Walter and Hafner's Jewelry Company in Hillsboro, the Katy's watch inspectors at that division point. Before the crash, thinking it would be good advertising, Walter had attached a long string to the watch and placed it in one of the locomotive's sandboxes. (An important component to any steam engine, the boxes held sand that could be dropped on the rails to improve traction when necessary.) The watch apparently had been left on the train by the jeweler for advertising purposes.

Despite complaints about how long it had taken the railroad to get all the spectators back on trains, the unnamed journalist from Austin, doubtless having traveled on the Katy's nickel to see the spectacle, had nothing negative to say about the railroad. "In connection with the great entertainment too much praise can not be said of the Katy management for the way in which they looked after the crowd on the grounds," he wrote.

As for the train delays, he continued, it was only natural that "there should be considerable mashing and jamming in trying to get trains back to town." That, however, "was the only defect in the whole day's pleasure, and this did not deter so very much when the novelty of the occasion is taken into consideration."

Not until several inches of type deep into his glowing story about the crash did the *Statesman* writer get around to mentioning "the sad turn affairs had taken in bringing about some wounded people on such a gala occasion." Considering the size of the crowd and all the confusion that followed, maybe the Austin journalist didn't yet realize just how bad it had been. Even as he wrote his story, three spectators lay dead as a direct or indirect result of the crash.

The more seriously injured spectators were put on the first train bound for the MKT passenger station in Waco. *Author's collection.*

John L. Overstreet and his wife mourned the loss of their fifteen-year-old daughter, Emma Frances Overstreet. The Overstreets farmed near Axtell, and like so many other locals, they had come in their wagon to see the collision. Not having ridden one of the excursion trains, they had seen the crash at no cost—not counting the death of one of their children.

Twenty-three-year-old Ernest L. Darnall (press reports following the crash incorrectly spelled his last name as "Darnell" and wrongly gave his age as nineteen) died in Waco's Pacific Hotel at 5:00 a.m., September 16, the morning after the crash. After suffering his injury, he never regained consciousness. As the *Austin Statesman* reported on September 17, a piece of chain, "driven like a cannon shot, crushed his skull." The young man had climbed up a mesquite tree to get a better view of the crash. Darnall's father, John W. Darnall, identified in the press only as "Colonel Darnell," came to Waco and returned with his son's body to Bremond. The small Robertson County community lay fifty-eight miles southeast of the crash site.

Crush's assistant said Ernest Darnall had been "warned no less than three times by officials of the company that if he remained [in the tree] he would be inviting death." A few days later, the *Sedalia Democrat* came to the Katy's defense as well. "With [one] exception...all the injured persons were on the east side of the track and outside of the grounds selected by the railroad...for the spectacle. Unparalleled recklessness was manifested by many people, and it is a matter of good fortune that more were not injured."

Two days after the crash, a young man who had been standing near Darnall when the two locomotives exploded paid a visit to the victim's brother-in-law at Calvert. Along with his condolences, he presented him with the chain that had killed his sister's husband. In contradiction to what Crush's assistant had said, he told Darnall's in-law that they had been about forty feet outside of the railroad's "dead line" when the trains met. A brief newspaper article about the macabre gift noted that the chain was about a foot long, was made of three-quarter-inch iron and weighed some eight to ten pounds. "There are blood stains on the chain," the September 19 *Dallas Morning News* article concluded.

John Morrison survived the crash, but not the event. After witnessing the spectacle, he and several friends, all from around the North Texas town of Ferris, managed to board the jammed first northbound special out of Crush. The train's passenger cars being filled well beyond capacity, he stood outside between the last coach and the caboose. Only a quarter mile from the crash scene, he fell from the train and the caboose's wheels crushed

Ernest Darnall died in a room in Waco's best hotel, the Pacific. Later, the hotel was renamed the Metropole. *Author's collection.*

his head "almost beyond recognition" and also severed his left arm. The conductor stopped the train and allowed two of Morrison's friends to get off and stay with his body beside the tracks pending the arrival of a justice of the peace to conduct an inquest. After the JP viewed the remains, the body was taken to Red Oak in Ellis County and from there to his home at Ferris, about twenty miles south of downtown Dallas.

The most seriously injured Crush survivor was photographer Jervis Deane, who had been struck in his right eye by a piece of the wreckage. The Austin newspaper listed the photographer's condition as "precarious." Louis Bergstrom, another of the photographers, had been injured but was expected to recover. The explosion's shock wave had knocked him down, but as the *Houston Post* put it, "the damage was slight."

Claude Alvey, described as "a prominent member of the volunteer fire department of Waco" and former city policeman, had sustained a serious chest injury after being struck by a flying piece of timber. He had been one of the two hundred special sheriff's deputies sworn in to help local law enforcement with the huge crowd. Fourteen-year-old Roy

Kendrick of Waco had been struck in his right ankle by a piece of metal that shattered bone.

As had the luckless Ernest Darnall, West area farmer Theodore Millenberger witnessed the crash from a tree he had climbed on the east side of the tracks. When a length of chain that had connected one of the engines to its coal tender struck the tree, it knocked Millenberger to the ground. In the fall, his left leg was broken and his right hip dislocated, and he suffered what the September 16 edition of the *Marshal (TX) Evening Messenger* called "an ugly scalp wound." The paper erroneously reported that he had died at 11:00 p.m. on September 15, but he survived.

W.T. Stamper, who lived near Granger in Williamson County, got hit on one of his hands by a piece of the wreckage. "The hand is badly swollen and very painful," the *Houston Post* reported, "but…physicians think that there were no bones fractured. Mr. Stamper has the missile as a souvenir of the collision." J.J. Sutterfield of Burleson was listed by the *Post* as having received a wound, but the newspaper offered no further details.

In Waxahachie, where an estimated five hundred residents had taken a train to see the crash, a cotton compress worker named John Besey was walking around with a bandage on his arm covering a severe laceration he had received from an airborne piece of metal. Making the best of a bad situation, he had picked up the object that struck him to keep as a souvenir.

Ardmore grocer G.W. Stuart had traveled all the way from Indian Territory to see the Crash at Crush. "He thinks the number of injured much greater than reported," the *Daily Ardmoreite* noted. "He says the only wonder to him is that there were not fifty to one hundred killed outright. He noticed a lone tree that presented the appearance of having received a charge of grapeshot."

When Crush reached Dallas the morning after the crash on his way to St. Louis, he gave a short statement to the *Dallas Morning News*:

> *I regret more than any person that anybody should have been injured as a result of the pre-arranged collisions. I certainly exerted all the resources at my command to keep the people beyond the danger line, but it was absolutely impossible.…*
>
> *As soon as I discovered that several people had been hurt I immediately took charge of the arrangements for their comfort and everything has been done for them that medical skill can accomplish. The death of young Darnell [sic] and the serious injury of others is the only cloud upon the success of the plan. Barring a few minor details everything was executed as*

Front-page story on crash in the September 16, 1896 edition of the *Galveston Daily News*. *Author's collection.*

intended, and I believe we had the largest crowd that ever assembled in this state. Of course no one could have foreseen that the explosion of the boilers would occur. Every possible precaution had been taken to guard against such a contingency, and we believed that it was almost impossible, but, in this as in many other cases, our plans miscarried to our very great regret.

The same day Crush's remarks were published, September 17, the *Galveston News* and its sister newspaper in Dallas printed comments from some of those who had witnessed the crash.

One of the more colorful characters on hand for the crash was Alex E. Sweet, publisher of *Texas Siftings*, a weekly humor newspaper. He took it all in from "afar off," he said, but had seen enough to last him for the rest of his life. "I would suggest to the enterprising caterers to the public fancy that the next thing in order ought to be a prearranged and carefully scheduled meeting of a waterspout and a tornado," Sweet quipped. "I am sure, from what I saw at Crush, that such a conjunction would draw a tremendous crowd and whet the jaded appetites of people who crave excitement."

While he had taken the spectacle in from what he considered a safe distance, Sweet told the *News* reporter he was still grateful to be alive. "When I saw the cap of the smokestack gently loitering in the atmosphere above me I heard it say, 'Come, Alex, come; you are too good for this earth,' but I told it the earth was not too good for me, and it grew offended and passed," the humorist said.

That piece, however, had not been the only missile that flew in his direction. "[A]nother aerial visitor in the shape of a solid chunk weighing about 20 pounds, sighted me and made signals by whistling that it desired to meet me," he said. "I was not feeling well and not thoroughly sure of the character and reputation of the whistler…[and]…declined an introduction and the visitor grew mad and dug a great hole in the ground not ten feet from [where] I stood."

Another spectator (the newspaper did not give his name), someone who had survived Pickett's Charge at Gettysburg during the Civil War and would carry the horror of that to his grave, said the locomotive explosions had been far more frightening than the bloody battle he had participated in. "I have been shot at 1,000,000 times, but the feeling was one of pleasure when I contrast it with my situation today," he said. "I have been wounded…and have been in a corner once or twice, but I have never got scared. Today when I saw those great chunks of iron and steel sailing around through the

Justice of the peace court docket book page showing disorderly conduct charge filed against one Crush spectator. *Photo by Mike Cox.*

air, grim demons seeking a victim, and realized my utter helplessness, I felt my heart go down in my boots."

Crush's chief clerk offered his thoughts: "I did not hear the falling pieces," Randolph Daniels said. "I admit I was pretty badly rattled for a few minutes and sought a place of safety. I have heard about collisions and read about them, but this one surpasses anything I had ever imagined."

His boss may not have liked reading what Daniels said next: "It [the collision] was too realistic to be comfortable." That said, suddenly the clerk saw things more corporately: "So far as the injured are concerned, I do not think a single soul was hurt who was beyond the dead line [the no-admittance safety zone]. A lot of excited people insisted on approaching to within 40 or 50 feet of the point of contact, and in spite of all the warnings and all the commands of the railroad officials and the constables they slipped in and were struck."

A tired, nervous Crush, meanwhile, arrived at the Katy's St. Louis offices on Thursday as ordered. He was told that T.C. Purdy, the railroad's vice-president and general manager, wanted to see him but was not yet available. The man who had planned the event that had gone so disastrously wrong sat and cooled his heels, not knowing what to expect but assuming he was about to be fired. Finally, he got in to see Purdy. Thirty-five years later, Crush described what happened next: "His first words, after we had exchanged greetings were: 'Crush, you are blameless.' My relief—well, I can't describe it, but you can imagine it."

THE PHOTOGRAPHERS

I n the romantic language of the late Victorian era, Jervis Corydon Deane made his living as a "shadow catcher," a man who "painted with light." A more prosaic way to put it was "itinerant photographer."

Born in Brooks County, Virginia (now West Virginia), in April 1860, he had three older brothers—Clarence C., Martin O. and Granville M.—all professional photographers. Early in his working life, before taking up the family trade, Jervis supported himself as a house painter in Hannibal, Missouri, where brother Clarence had a photography studio. From the Mississippi River town made famous by Mark Twain, in 1885 Jervis traveled to Europe to study photography so he could join his siblings in the family calling. He later noted that his study abroad had been "not only [to] please his…patrons, but to advance the science of photography."

Curly haired and with a fashionable, drooping mustache, Deane was a worldly, serious-looking young man who apparently was not put off by the notion of hard work. However, it did seem difficult for him to stay in one place very long. Back in the States, he plied his new trade at various places around the country, often working with one of his brothers. Following the money, or at least the possibility of making money, he hit Waco, Texas, around 1887. He partnered with another photographer named Forrest T. Morgan, forming the firm of Deane & Morgan. In addition to operating in Waco, they had studios in East Texas at Palestine and Jefferson. They remained partners until 1891.

Jervis C. Deane and his brothers believed in the power of newspaper advertising. *Author's collection.*

Deane clearly believed in the power of newspaper advertising, but he did it on the cheap, buying two- or three-line ads like this one that ran on August 16, 1888, in the *Waco Evening News*: "For first class Photos of all styles, call on Deane, Waco's high priced Photographer. No cheap shoddy work done." Always referring to himself simply as "Deane," he sometimes had as many as fifteen such short ads scattered through a particular edition. Only occasionally would he pay for a larger, costlier display ad.

The same year he went into business in Waco, Deane entered another form of partnership on October 31, 1887, when he married Maude F. Hillin, the daughter of a local carriage maker. One year later, the couple had a son, Jervis C. Deane Jr. Two years after that, in November 1890, Maude gave birth to a daughter, Karma, and another son the following year, Peyton.

Deane's studio was located downtown at 414½ Austin Avenue. The Waco City Directory for 1888–89 described his place of business as "ornamented with his artistic work, and where he has every facility and modern improvement to enable him to properly carry on his business."

Cameras being bulky and heavy, Deane did almost all of his work in his studio. But he was far more portable than his photography equipment. In 1894, Deane and his young family relocated to Fort Worth, where he opened a studio at 610 Main Street. The same year, one of his small ads in the *Fort Worth Gazette* noted that he had won first place in photography at the "Dallas Exposition," an early name for the State Fair of Texas. The Deanes remained in Fort Worth through April 1896, when they moved back to Waco.

J.C. Deane three years before the crash. For a man who made his living taking pictures, he did not pose for many himself. *Author's collection.*

Whether based on Deane's reputation for producing good work or simply the luck of the draw, that summer William Crush approached him about being the official still photographer for the coming locomotive crash on the Katy line. The railroad being a corporation with accountants and lawyers, a contract was probably executed between the two, although no copy has been located in surviving MKT records. Crush likely offered Deane a flat fee, with Deane retaining the right to sell prints of the photographs he would be taking before, at the moment of and after the crash. The Katy also may have asked for a percentage of his print sales.

Deane asked his brothers Martin and Granville to help him with the shoot. He also hired Waco photographer Louis Bergstrom to assist them at the crash site. On the day of the event, they set up three cameras on the elevated stand built for the photographers. "At the time of the collision he [Jervis] was ready for the picture and he completed it just as the steel bolt entered his eye," Maude Deane told a reporter. "His brothers then took up the work and went on with it." Bergstrom also captured one or more images before the crash.

How much money the photographers netted is not known, but the venture nearly cost Jervis Deane his life and left him with only one eye—a significant disability for anyone, more so for a man who made his living looking through a camera lens.

Bergstrom later recalled that after the explosion, which knocked him and Deane down, Deane got up with blood coming out of the corner of one of his eyes. Still, plainly operating on adrenaline, Deane gave his brothers "minute directions about the finishing of the pictures he had taken." Realizing that Deane was hurt, Bergstrom yelled out for a doctor. Gripping his black medical bag, a physician identified only as Dr. Wederwich fought his way through the throng and attended to the injured photographer as best he could. "I rushed to the platform and found my husband in the hands of the surgeons," Maude Deane told a reporter. "They were administering anesthetics hypodermically and he was going to sleep nicely."

Two days after the crash, the *Galveston News* reported that Deane probably wouldn't survive. "The other Waco sufferers will recover, except Photographer J.C. Deane, who is in a precarious situation," the newspaper pronounced. The unnamed journalist then offered graphic details on the man's injury: "The force of the boiler explosion drove a bolt three-fourths of an inch thick and two and one-half inches long straight into his eye, hitting the center and dissolving the eyeball. The bolt went nut foremost, piercing the orbital plate and injuring the brain." When doctors first examined Deane, they had not even realized that the missile that had destroyed his eye remained in his skull. "It was hidden… entirely," the newspaper continued, "buried out of sight. Its presence [only] became known when the probe was inserted." The article went on to note that the surgeon who treated Deane had declared that "recovery in such cases is the exception." Granville Deane said he had been told Jervis's chance of survival was only 10 percent.

Not realizing that his brother had been as seriously injured as he was, Granville Deane returned to Dallas the night of the collision. He told the *Dallas Morning News* that he had at first been reluctant to get on the photography platform but that he had been assured it would be safe. "He added that he desired no more collision pictures," the newspaper said.

Even as Jervis Deane lay recovering from surgery, the *Waco Tribune* continued publishing an ad he had paid for prior to the crash. It boasted that "Deane, The Photographer," had taken "First Premium over all competitors at the Temper flower show for Best Photos on exhibition. Fine Photographic work a specialty. NO CHEAP WORK."

Deane beat the odds. "My husband is all right except the loss of his eye," Maude Deane told a reporter a few weeks later. "His brain is not impaired and he is anxious to resume his work." On October 3, the *Houston Post* published a short article headlined, "Deane's Wonderful Recovery." The photographer "came downtown in his carriage yesterday [October 1] and is

Having gotten all the loose screws and other hardware out of my head, am now ready for all

PHOTOGRAPHIC BUSINESS.

Waco's High-Priced Photographer.

Ad Deane placed in a Waco newspaper to let his customers know he was back in business after recovering from the injury he suffered at Crush. *Author's collection.*

almost well enough to resume his business," the story said. His wound had been "healing rapidly and has been ever since the bolt was withdrawn."

Crush had said the collision would be a contribution to science, and thanks to Deane, in a small way it was. His lead physician, Dr. Garland B. Foscue, reported on the case at the next meeting of the Central Texas Medical Association.

Whatever else made up his personality, Deane possessed a sense of humor. When he had recovered sufficiently to go back to work, he did so sporting a new glass eye and placed this ad in a local newspaper: "Having gotten all the loose screws and other hardware out of my head, am now ready for all photographic business."

At some point following the crash that nearly killed Jervis, the brothers Deane produced and sold a set of striking images they took that day. Each print was mounted on cardboard and bore a credit line reading, "Photograph by Deane of DALLAS, FORT WORTH, Waco and Houston." (Why they uppercased Dallas and Fort Worth and not the other two cities is anyone's guess.) The first photograph, captioned "Shaking Hands," shows the two locomotives facing each other before the crash. The next image, "The Trains Just as They Struck," pictured the two engines racing toward each other only a few feet apart, black smoke pouring from their old-fashioned diamond stacks. The third image, "The Explosion," captures the moment of impact and the boiler explosions that followed. The fourth image, "Before the Crowd Got to the Wreck," shows the scene only moments after the impact. Finally, "The Crowd at the Wreck," shows a sea of humanity sweeping over the scene.

Since Jervis Deane would have been out of action after the explosion, the last two images must have been taken by one of his brothers or Bergstrom. How many of these images Deane printed and sold is not known, but only two sets of prints are known to have survived. Nor is it known how much

Deane sold the prints for, but a newspaper ad published in Fort Worth earlier that year noted that his portrait prints went for $2.95 each.

Some accounts of the crash and its aftermath have Deane receiving $10,000 and a lifetime pass from the Katy in compensation for his injury, but if that happened, it was a voluntary action on the part of the railroad. McLennan County district court dockets do not show that Deane filed suit against the railroad.

While Deane was well known in Waco, Enoch J. Rector, the man invited by Crush to make a moving picture of the staged collision, would gain international recognition as one of the key figures in the development of cinematography.

Like Deane, Rector was a West Virginian. Born in Parkersburg during the Civil War, his childhood was less than idyllic. His mother died when he was young, and he did not get along particularly well with his stepmother or her son, his stepbrother. In fact, he later told his granddaughter that he had accidentally killed one of his brothers with a bow and arrow and run away to join a circus. While research has shown he had nothing to do with the deaths of his biological siblings, the jury is still out on whether he killed the stepbrother with a flying arrow.

If he did travel with a circus for a time, he went on to attend West Virginia University in 1883, and while he did not earn a degree, he received a good education heavy on the sciences and the emerging field of electrical engineering. Though not specifically trained in civil engineering, after leaving the university in 1885 he got a job with the Northern Pacific Railroad. Late in the following year, he went by ship from Seattle to Buenos Aires to work on a railroad construction project extending from Brazil to Bolivia. While he was in the Brazilian state of Mato Grosso, a revolution broke out and he returned to the United States in the latter part of 1891.

Back in the United States, on the heels of a failed manufacturing venture in Tennessee, Rector went to New York. There, in 1894, he teamed up with Otway Latham to form a company with an innovative business model—they would make moving pictures of prizefights for exhibition on Kinetoscopes.

Invented by Thomas Edison, the Kinetoscope was a machine that played a silent, moving film that could be viewed—for pay—through a peephole. The camera, which captured images frame by frame to produce a moving picture, was called a Kintograph. At the Edison studio in Orange, New Jersey, the company filmed a boxing match between "Gentleman" Jim Corbett and underdog Peter Courtney. The company went on to exhibit each of the six,

When Enoch J. Rector tried to film the Fitzsimmons-Maher prizefight near Langtry, Texas, he used a camera half the size of a railroad box car. *Author's collection.*

one-minute rounds as separate peepshows, the segments collectively known as "Corbett and Courtney Before the Kintograph."

A year and a half later, Rector traveled to Texas to film the much-touted and as equally denounced prizefight pitting Bob Fitzsimmons against challenger Peter Maher. Nine days before the bout, which would take place on an island in the Rio Grande near Langtry, Texas, Rector and his associates slipped out of El Paso to set up his cameras, a process that involved putting up a wooden structure with a window for each of the four battery-powered cameras. Not quite half the length of a railroad box car, essentially it was a giant dark room on stilts, complete with a red glass skylight to allow Rector and his helpers to see inside without exposing their film. The fight lasted only one round, but Rector emerged from his camera shack with a roll of film. Unfortunately for him and his company, thanks to an overcast sky, the film did not turn out.

Back in El Paso, he came up with a way to transform the proverbial sow's ear into a silk matador's cape by successfully filming a violent contest of another sort—a bull fight across the border in Juarez, Mexico. Interviewed by the *Dallas Morning News* on his way back to New York, Rector said he had been successful "in photographing the most bloody and exciting bull fight of the series which took place after the pugilistic contest." When asked if he "or the Kinetoscope people" had put up the purse for the dud prizefight on the border, the movie man laughed. "Our contract with Mr. [Dan] Stuart was entirely on a percentage basis, as we could not afford to pay any cash for the right to photograph the fight." Their risk, he said, had been in bringing $17,000 worth of equipment to far West Texas. Had it not been for the bullfight, he said, he would have suffered "a clear loss."

Back in New York, his company did not survive the failure to get the Fitzsimmons fight on film. But soon he partnered with Stuart and organized a new venture, the Kineto-Multiscope Company, in April 1896. While Stuart busied himself trying to arrange a fight between Fitzsimmons and Corbet, Rector decided that the Edison cameras he had been using were impractical and designed his own camera. His camera was hand-cranked and would use a new, more sensitive film recently developed by Eastman Kodak.

Rector tried his new camera at Alfred Streeter's prearranged crash in Ohio on May 30, 1896. If he succeeded in capturing the nation's first staged train collision on film, it is not known to have survived. When Crush started planning his Texas collision, remembering what he had read in the newspaper about Rector's arrangement with the boxing promoter may have been what led the Katy official to contact him about filming the locomotive crash that summer. Likely Crush offered the same sort of deal fight promoter Stuart had. On the other hand, Rector might have reached out to Crush when word of the planned Texas smashup began to spread.

The explosion following the collision at Crush did not injure Rector, and the outcome of his filming is unknown. If he succeeded in filming the first prearranged train crash west of the Mississippi, the footage has been lost. More likely his camera got knocked over by the shock wave from explosions or even damaged to the extent that it leaked light and ruined the film. Since there was no subsequent newspaper coverage mentioning that the Crush crash had been filmed, it seems unlikely that Rector returned to New York with any usable footage.

Interviewed by a reporter soon after the crash, Rector did come up with a passable word picture of what happened when the boilers blew. "I have

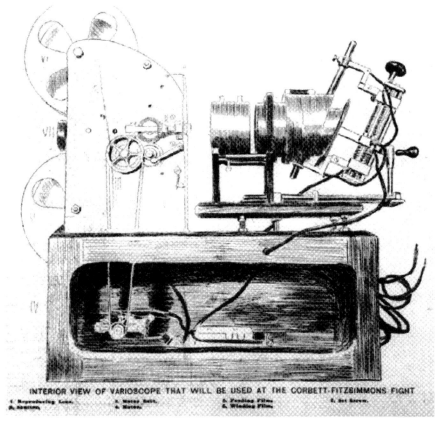

INTERIOR VIEW OF VARIOSCOPE THAT WILL BE USED AT THE CORBETT-FITZSIMMONS FIGHT

New York moviemaker Enoch J. Rector used a machine similar to this to film the Crash at Crush. The footage either did not turn out or has been lost. *Author's collection.*

seen a great many things in my life, and have had some pretty close calls, but that [the collision] knocks anything cold that I have ever seen before," he told a reporter for the *Galveston News*. "I saw the collision on the Hocking Valley road [the Ohio crash]…and that was not a marker to this one. I doubt if there was ever more complete destruction in the world than of those two engines. I went over and looked at the wreck after it was all over and it did not seem to me as if a piece of one of the engines as big as a hat remained."

Rector had been standing on the photography platform with Deane and the other photographers when "the rain of iron and steel began falling." When a large chunk of iron flew in his direction, he continued, "I made up my mind that it was all day with me and got down on my knees behind the machine [his large movie camera]." The metal, which he said appeared to be "as big as the whole state of Texas," passed within four feet of him and fell just behind the platform. The injured Jervis Deane's brother Granville said, "There is not money enough in the country to get me on one again.… The whistling of the fragments of iron and steel as they swept by me made an impression I will never forget."

The images the brothers Deane and their assistant, Louis Bergstrom, took of the Crash at Crush that day amount to the only known photographic documentation of the weird and tragic event that took place in Central Texas that summer afternoon in 1896.

LITIGATION AHEAD

Like hundreds, if not thousands, of the people who witnessed the staged train crash and the twin explosions that followed, Billy McBride was poking around the soon-to-be ghost town of Crush later that afternoon looking for a suitable piece of debris to keep as a souvenir.

As people crowded onto a steady stream of outbound excursion trains, the Hillsboro resident noticed a burlap bag stuffed under the wooden platform adjacent to the depot. When he pulled the bag away, he found a wooden box containing 150 sticks of what looked to him like dynamite.

News of the discovery did not get out until Thursday, September 17, when a Hillsboro newspaper noted the find in an article that some of the state's morning newspapers reprinted the following day. That afternoon, Friday the eighteenth, the *Dallas Times-Herald* ran an inside story headlined "Dynamite." The articled sparked a short-lived conspiracy theory that may have briefly cheered Katy's already lawsuit-leery management: perhaps the explosions that followed the Crash at Crush had been the work of a saboteur, not a matter of negligence on the part of the railroad.

"In a circle of men…discussing the event this morning," the newspaper said, "was a well known business man of this city, an eye witness of the collision, who said: 'It is not only possible, but highly probable, that some person with evil and malicious intent placed sticks of dynamite on the colliding engines, which caused the explosion. Anarchists are broadcast in the land, and an opportunity is never missed by the more rabid ones to do all the damage possible, and the collision at Crush…offered a splendid and what must have seemed to them a safe opportunity for this kind of work.'"

Despite the certitude expressed in his comment, the owner of this theory apparently asked that his name not be published. The man continued: "This is the first instance in the history of [deliberate locomotive] collisions where the boilers exploded, and when I think of the extraordinary precautions taken on this occasion to prevent an explosion, the more firmly am I convinced that this is the work of some nefarious dynamiter or some green country hunk of a boy who wanted some fun, never thinking of the consequences."

Apparently, no one else took the dynamite story seriously. More than likely, what McBride found was an unused box of railroad signal fusees. While dangerous to someone who did not know how to use them properly, the slender tubes produced a bright flame, not an explosion.

Few people, aside from those mourning their dead or worrying about their injured family members, seemed particularly bothered that Crush's crash had killed or maimed innocent bystanders in the name of money and free publicity for the MKT. The majority of the state's newspapers expressed no outrage and, if anything, downplayed the boiler explosions and the havoc they wreaked. In fact, several published accounts of the crash blamed the spectators, not the Katy.

The *Houston Post*, however, led its first article after the crash with the news that people had died. "The great head end collision resulted disastrously," the newspaper began. "It was a huge success as a collision but it spread havoc around it."

Another exception among the state's mainstream media was the *San Antonio Light*, one of two dailies in what was then Texas's second-largest city. "There is going to be trouble with the settlement of the damage suits arising out of that duel between the engines at Crush, near Waco," the newspaper editorialized on September 21. "While the Katy did all that seemed necessary to do in the way of precautions against accident, it seems that the force of the explosion was not accurately gauged and that the missiles were hurled much farther than was calculated upon."

The Alamo City newspaper did note that the situation likely had been aggravated by "people…crowding within the limits [the safety perimeter that the railroad had failed to preserve]." Litigation that had already been filed, as well as cases likely to be brought, "will present some nice points of law." The San Antonio editorial concluded, "No doubt out of it all the end will be that such exhibitions in this country will not be repeated, and this will be well."

Closer to the scene of the crash, the editor of the *Tribune*, one of Waco's three dailies, offered sympathy to the families of the victims but maintained, "Thousands of people would have been reckless enough to go to the scene of the tragedy even with good reason to believe, beforehand, that a sad outcome would ensue." For the Katy, the editorial had stronger words: "It was purely a speculation and advertising scheme so far as the railway is concerned, and if it has to pay roundly for lives lost and human suffering the verdict of the public will be: 'served it right.'"

The same edition of the *Tribune* carried a report from its country correspondent in Axtell that included an even stronger comment from crash witness James Casey: "I believe the state or county officers should have seen that everybody not immediately concerned [in staging the crash] was at a safe distance. While it was a scene to be remembered, while life lasts, still sober second thought tells me that this thing was very close to deliberate murder. And I hope that congress will prohibit anything of the kind hereafter in the United States."

Casey dismissed William Crush's claim that the crash would benefit science. "After viewing the 'wreck' I doubt that a [railroad] car builder could learn enough by a thorough examination of it to do him $100 worth of good! All the rolling stock, on all the railroads in Texas, is not worth one dollar compared to the worth of one of the victims' lives. The writer took his chances at about 200 yards distance and believes he knows what he's talking about."

Among the state's smaller newspapers, less than forty miles from the scene of the crash in the Bosque County town of Clifton, the weekly *Record* was much harsher. "The great wreck of trains at Crush…was advertised to be for scientific purposes," the newspaper began. "Possibly a limited knowledge of railroad affairs forbids some people [from] seeing the real science there was in the wreck. When it is known that more than 30,000 people gathered to witness the destruction, that the land for three miles around was leased by railroad management and that no one was allowed to come in except by rail, it may be seen that it was a scientific way of disposing of worn out rolling stock for more than enough [money] to purchase anew."

Pointing out that several had been injured and some killed by the explosion following the crash, the newspaper judged that "the homes that are darkened and the hearts that are sadden[ed] by the death of loved ones will see no ray of light from such a scientific collision." The piece concluded with another infusion of editorial venom: "The wounded who may in [the] future go about with blind eyes or an empty sleeve asking alms of an uncharitable public, will hardly point with pride to the Crush wreck and say, 'there by science I lost my sight, my leg or my arm and I am unfitted to earn my bread.'"

By far the worst printed criticism, to the point of being acerbic, came in a weekly, four-page Waco publication called *Artesia*. Published by Isaac A. Goldstein, owner of the city's largest dry goods store, the *Artesia* did not normally cover hard news. Clearly intended for the society set, the three-thousand-circulation weekly featured items mostly of interest to women, from the latest in fashion to coming "hops" (dances) and other social and club activities. The September 30 edition, however, amounted to a sardonic slap of Katy's face:

CARNIVAL OF DEATH
How Railroad Royalty Amuses Itself

The great M., K. & T. show last Tuesday recalls with life-like vividness the storied festivities of ancient Rome and Greece. Since human slaves were devoured by wild animals in the circus at Rome, and Christian priests were slain by gladiators to amuse the populace, such scenes have not been known. For the paltry consideration of a few thousand dollars every device was used to gather an immense congregation of men, women and children to witness a show advertised as harmless, but which in the very nature of such things was dangerous to the highest degree. This danger was known to the railroad people, for they drew a dead-line and warned the heedless multitude that death waited for his victims on the other side; and death had his harvest. The multitude, debauched with beer and debased with the sight of blood, cried for more. The managers express themselves highly pleased with their little fun; the "free press" are full of glowing accounts of the wonderful and successful exhibition, unparalleled in the history of Texas; and the dead and wounded are forgotten in the excitement of the brutalizing sport.

The great Katy collision excursion was a success! True, some hundred people were seriously injured, but none of the railroad capitalists were harmed. Four or five lives were lost, but only their relatives and friends will mourn. Several thousand dollars went out of Waco to see the murder done, but if it had not been thrown into the Katy's hungry maw it might have been wasted on a dam or other home enterprise. Yes, the collision was a success—a few mothers and wives are crying over their dead, but the merry railroad magnates are bowling along in special cars and viewing the splendors and profits of the wreck through cheerful clouds of Havana smoke. Look for the next excursion date, all ye who are tired and weary of life!

Justice indeed seems blind and humanity heartless, when we consider how little regard is given for the life and safety of the people. A prominent lawyer speaking of the sad calamity last Tuesday, said: "It is one of the most shameless and heartless abuses of public franchise ever known. Railroads are chartered for transportation purposes only, and have no more legal right to exhibit a show than they would have to go into the banking business. It was a willful violation of the laws for public safety, and somebody should be held to strict accountability for such wanton jeopardy of human life. The grand jury could not do the people better service than to investigate the matter and bring to punishment the reckless perpetrators of this outrage."

A few out-of-state newspapers also weighed in with some criticism. "Head-end collisions for a show and to make money may not be as demoralizing as prize fighting," opined the *Daily Ardmoreite* in Oklahoma Territory, "but from the result of yesterday's demonstration in that line they are equally, if not more dangerous to the spectators. It is now in order for Gov. Culberson of Texas, to call an extra session of his legislature to pass a law against a repetition of such occurrences."

The governor must not have subscribed to the Ardmore newspaper. The Texas legislature did not convene until January 20, 1897, which was for a regular session. A thirty-day special session did follow in Austin that May 21, but if a lawmaker introduced a bill banning the deliberate crashing of locomotives, the measure did not make it out of the figurative roundhouse.

The Oklahoma editorial writer proved more accurate in the other observation he made the day after the crash: "Besides the crush of engines at Crush, Texas, yesterday, there were several crushed heads and before it is done with Mr. Crush is liable to have his pocket book crushed for damages." In Texas, the *Shiner Gazette* agreed. "By the time the M.K.& T. get [*sic*] through paying damages to the persons injured in the Crush collision," the weekly opined on September 24, "it will not have enough left to buy those two new engines."

Compared with the coverage newspapers gave to the crash's run-up and the catastrophic consequences that followed the collision, the legal tussle between the families of some of the victims and the railroad received only slight mention.

Only four days after the collision, John L. Overstreet filed suit against the MKT, seeking $16,300 in actual and punitive damages in the death of his daughter. The plaintiff's petition said Miss Overstreet, who had been standing 375 yards (1,125 feet) to the rear of the crash site, had been

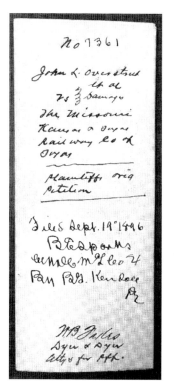

John L. Overstreet and his wife filed a lawsuit against the Katy shortly after their fifteen-year-old daughter was killed in the explosion following the Crash at Crush. *Author's collection.*

struck by a piece of timber 2 feet long, 4 inches wide and 2 inches thick. The blow had crushed her skull. The "grievous loss of their beloved child & daughter" deprived him of his daughter's labor on the farm, the value of that amounting to $200 a year for the six years until she would have attained her majority. Also noted in the petition was that her funeral expenses had been $100. Those two loses came to $1,300, with the balance sought as punitive damages.

In the Katy's headquarters city, the September 20 edition of the *Dallas Morning News* afforded the lawsuit only two paragraphs. "This action will test the liability of the railway company in the accidents occurring at the collision," the article concluded.

Waco attorneys George Clark and D.C. Bollinger of the law firm of Clark, Dyer and Bollinger soon filed a demurrer (now generally referred to as a denial) on behalf of the Katy on October 3. "By way of special exception," they wrote, "defendant says that the defendant is sued as a railway corporation, a common carrier, and that the acts of negligence and various torts and wrongs complained of were done and committed by agents, officers and employes [*sic*] of said railway corporation while acting entirely out of the line [meaning not in their capacity as railroad employees] and powers of such officers, agents and employees of the defendant's corporation."

In other words, the lawyers were asserting, presumably with a straight face, that the MKT was not responsible for any alleged "acts of negligence" because it was a corporation, not a person. Even the railway line's employees, the answer seems to argue, had not been acting on behalf of their corporation. As the *Dallas Morning News* reported, the railroad "denies that [it] had anything to do with the collision and declares that it is not responsible in any manner for the accident, which destroyed the life of Miss Overstreet."

Beyond that, the Katy's answer continued, "it appears from plaintiff's petition that the said Emma Frances Overstreet was injured and killed while

Right: Katy attorney George W. Clark of Waco prepared general denials in response to the two lawsuits filed against the MKT following the crash, but the railroad ended up settling the two cases. *Author's collection.*

Below: The damage suits against the Katy were filed with the district clerk at the McLennan County Courthouse in Waco but are now in storage at the McLennan County Archives. *Author's collection.*

a witness to an entertainment exhibition alleged to have been given by the said agents, officers and employees of the defendant's corporation," but in truth "said entire exhibition and acts and conduct of said officers, agents and employees, as appear from the plaintiff's petition, were wholly unauthorized and beyond their power and scope of authority; that the defendant, in the nature of things, as a railway corporation, was not authorized in law to do any such business or conduct any such performance."

Just in case the court didn't buy their *ultra vires* argument (that the alleged acts were beyond the scope of the corporation as defined by its charter), the lawyers proceeded in their answer with a general denial. They claimed that the victim was not there "at defendant's invitation, that she was killed on land not controlled by the defendant, and that the defendant had no control over the events that transpired and therefore could not be held responsible for her death."

The Katy's answer received only perfunctory newspaper coverage, and the next development did not get any mention at all in the press. No records have been found shedding light on whether any negotiation occurred between the lawyers involved or whether the MKT management simply came to understand that it would be bad form (and even worse PR) for the railroad if the case went to trial before a jury. When Overstreet's attorney subpoenaed ten witnesses to appear in Nineteenth Judicial District Court on November 5 the Katy's attorneys apparently concluded that it would be in the best interest of their client to settle, and that's what happened. The railroad paid the full amount the Overstreets had sought.

Wacoan John D. Kendrick filed suit against the Katy on November 11 on behalf of his minor son, Roy. The plaintiff's petition said the teenager had suffered a fractured right ankle when hit by a piece of flying debris following the crash and that he had been unable to walk and in considerable pain ever since. In recompense, the father sought $500 in damages. Again, the Waco law firm representing the railroad filed a one-page, two-paragraph answer the following day denying "all and singular the allegations, matters and things in plaintiff's petition." The same day, however, recently seated Nineteenth Judicial District judge Marshall Surratt entered a judgment against the railroad awarding the damages sought by Kendrick on behalf of his son plus court costs.

Later tellings of the Crash at Crush story have the Katy sued by all the victims or their survivors, but district court records in McLennan County reveal only two cases filed, the one by Overstreet and the one by Kendrick. The common story line is that all those injured by the crash received $10,000 and a lifetime pass from the Katy, but that seems highly unlikely. There is certainly no known documentation to support that.

Despite the railroad's legal fees and the money spent on settlements, the Katy was doing well financially. "The M.K.&T. in spite of the general depression in railroad affairs, continues to pile up good earnings," the *Parsons (KS) Daily Sun* reported on September 26. "The figures for the second week in September are $291,030, an increase of $57,528.97 over the corresponding period last year." While earnings connected to the Crush crash would not have shown up until the week three figures came in, thanks to the event the line doubtless saw a revenue bump. In fact, the company's annual report, released a few weeks later, showed gross passenger service earnings of $1,206,803.34 for September 1896, compared with $1,055,267.96 in September 1895. Overall, for the twelve months beginning on June 30, 1896, the Katy reported gross revenue of $4,354,829. Of thirty-six Texas lines reporting to the state's Railroad Commission, only two had out-earned the MKT.

"There is a well defined rumor in railway circles that the [MKT] is soon to add a number of new passenger engines to its already large stock, that has, so the rumor says, proved insufficient for the transactions of the road's business," the *Houston Post* reported that October 31. The newspaper went on to say that the new engines would be equipped with electric headlights. The article offered no source for the rumored plans to buy new rolling stock, but the information clearly came from someone with the Katy, possibly Crush. Whoever wrote the story made no effort to be objective: "It is gratifying to state that in President Rouse's recent annual statement, the Katy is free of floating debt, which naturally lends color the rumor. With a number of new passenger engines equipped with the electric headlight, the [MKT] would possess motive power second to none in the South."

Less than a month after the smashup, Crush traveled to Louisville to visit family and, as the *Louisville Courier-Journal* put it, had been "calling on his numerous old friends." Clearly, politics was the main thing on Crush's mind. "Mr. Crush wears a McKinley button and declares that Texas will not give her electoral vote to Bryan by a long shot," the brief article in his hometown newspaper noted. Moving on from the impending presidential election, "Mr. Crush declares the Lone Star State to be the best in the Union for railroads. The people travel extensively. He had a crowd of 75,000 to see a collision of two locomotives recently."

If the tragic results of the crash he had conceived and coordinated bothered him, the comments he made to his hometown newspaper did not betray the fact. Not only did he not seem to regret the deadly outcome of the event, but Crush had also exaggerated even the largest reported estimate of the crowd by 50 percent.

Back in Texas, Crush went about his job with his usual confident, positive nature, always speaking of the Katy as glowingly as he would of his sisters or mother. "General Passenger and Ticket Agent Crush of the Katy came down from Dallas last night, looking after the business of his department," the *Houston Post* noted on November 19. "Mr. Crush says that the Katy is in first class shape, doing a fine business and promises to continue so."

THE KING OF RAGTIME

About a month after the deadly extravaganza at Crush, a serious-looking, well-dressed black man walked into a music store on the first floor of a two-story brick building at South Main and Avenue A in Temple, a flourishing railroad town south of Waco.

Proprietor Robert Smith and salesman Jack Fuller greeted Scott Joplin, leader of a musical group called the Texas Medley Quartette. At first the men may have thought Joplin had come by to see how sales of his "Harmony Club Waltz" and "Combination March" were going, but that wasn't his business on this fall day. The musician told them he had a third composition he hoped Smith would consider publishing and marketing.

Joplin and his fellow musicians had been in town for a month or so, playing some of the rowdy clubs on nearby Eighth Street, the main drag running through the black part of town. Temple had a sizable population of African Americans, many employed by the two rail lines serving the city—the Katy and the Santa Fe. While African Americans earned considerably less than their white coworkers and mostly held the hard-labor jobs, with the railroads they had steady employment at union rates. They spent much of their money along Eighth Street, which was lined with black-owned stores, groceries, churches, funeral homes, boardinghouses, clubs and saloons. Whether Smith or Fuller had ever seen Joplin and his fellow music men perform is not known, but they surely were aware of the ensemble's growing reputation. And Joplin's sheet music was selling well at their store.

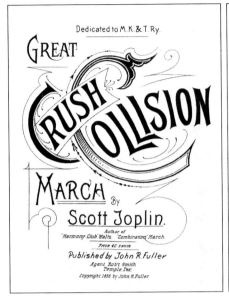

Left: Sheet music for the "Great Crush Collision March" was published by a Temple, Texas music store for budding ragtime musician Scott Joplin. *Author's collection.*

Right: First page of Joplin's composition, written and published in Temple, Texas, within weeks of the Crash at Crush. *Author's collection.*

Joplin said that he had composed a march commemorating the recent Crash at Crush. No records are known reflecting on the nature of the deal they struck, but Smith, who had been selling pianos and other musical instruments in Temple for three years, was more than happy to cash in on all the ink and talk the recent Katy stunt had generated. Job printers were available in Temple, but salable sheet music required ornate, eye-catching typography that could only be accomplished through a copperplate engraving process. That took an overall level of expertise the local shops lacked. Soon, Joplin's new score was in the mail to 182 High Holburn Street in London, the printing firm of Charles Sheard & Company. With sound recording and player piano rolls still in their infancy, the only way a musician could make money beyond performing in front of an audience was to sell his original pieces or adaptations as sheet music. The British firm that had printed Joplin's earlier two works was enjoying considerable success in publishing African American music (either black songs or compositions by black musicians) in addition to more traditional genres.

For a man whose work was being produced by one of the world's better-known sheet music houses, Joplin's early life had not held much promise in the racially charged era during which he grew up—at least not until a German-born music tutor realized that young Joplin possessed musical genius.

Joplin was born on a tenant farm near the Northeast Texas town of Linden, in what is now Cass County. (His accepted date of birth is November 24, 1868, but Joplin's biographer notes there is no hard proof of his birthday, which could have been in 1867 and not necessarily on the day usually shown.) His father, Giles, a former slave, played the fiddle, and his mother, Florence, sang and played the banjo. Growing up in a musical family, Joplin learned to play by ear. By seven, he was strumming a banjo, sawing a fiddle and rattling the keys of a piano.

In 1875, Joplin's father got a railroad job in Texarkana and moved the family there. To add to their income, Florence did cleaning and washing for white families. One of the people she worked for was an attorney who didn't mind if she let her son Scott practice on his family's piano. She also worked at the home of Robert W. Rodgers, a wealthy lumberman who employed a tutor for his children. That tutor, Julius Weiss, gave Joplin free piano lessons and taught him to read music. When Rodgers died in 1884, Weiss left Texarkana. Teenage Joplin left too, though exactly when has never been pinned down.

The generally accepted story is that after a disagreement with his father (who left Florence for another woman), young Joplin left home somewhere between 1884 and 1888 to make his own way as a roving musician. Supporting himself as a "piano thumper" in brothels and saloons, he traveled in Texas, Louisiana, Missouri, Illinois, Ohio and Kentucky before landing in St. Louis around 1890. His steadiest gig in the robust metropolis on the Mississippi River was at the Silver Dollar Saloon, which is where he first began playing "jig piano," a fast style that soon became known as "ragged time" and, finally, "ragtime."

Despite the less-than-savory environments where he made music, Joplin had begun to demonstrate that he had an innate talent worthy of a higher-class clientele. He spent some time back in Texarkana in 1891, playing with a black minstrel group before moving to Sedalia, Missouri—a prosperous former cattle town and MKT division point known as the "Queen City of the Prairies." There he organized an ensemble with younger brothers Will and Robert and five other black musicians. Only three of them are known to have hailed from the Lone Star State, and there were eight in the group, not four, but they called themselves the Texas Medley Quartette.

At first, the troupe mostly played plantation songs and minstrel tunes, a genre even African Americans then referred to as "Coon Music." But Joplin soon would be writing his own pieces, and in time, the form of music he and other black musicians of his generation pioneered would transcend racial differences. Their work would lead to the emergence of blues music, which led to the various varieties of jazz, which led to swing, which led to rock.

In Sedalia, Joplin became acquainted with Henry "Pleasant" Jackson, a porter with the MKT. On passenger runs, like all African American porters, Jackson wore a starched white coat and tended to the needs of white travelers in the Pullman or dining cars. But when he wasn't on a run, he could often be found playing with the Quartette in one of Sedalia's tawdry East Main Street joints, places like the Black 400 Club and the Maple Leaf Club.

Despite being relegated to segregated passenger coaches, it was easy enough for the Texas Medley Quartette to travel from Sedalia across the country, playing wherever they could hustle a gig. When the Chicago World's Fair opened in the spring of 1893, Joplin went there to play the black "sporting houses" near the fairgrounds. How many other members of the Quartette accompanied him to Illinois is not known, but they did continue to play as a group after the exposition ended.

"The Texas Medley Quartette is in town," the *St. Paul (MN) Globe* reported in the fall of 1893, "and is giving some splendid vocal music in the public buildings and in office buildings having large courts. The people who hear the quartet manifest their appreciation of a good thing in music by showering silver upon its members."

Playing in Boston in September 1894, the quartet showed up at the newsroom of the *Boston Herald* and offered staffers a free performance. The newspaper obliged the group with a short article, "Herald Folk Serenaded," in which whoever wrote the three-paragraph item noted the Medley Quartette's performance of "several well chosen selections…[had been] rendered in a very artistic manner." The piece also noted that the group had been traveling through the West for several years, but that this was their first visit to the East Coast. The following year, in Syracuse, New York, Joplin got his first two pieces of music published.

With a significant part of Sedalia's population associated in one way or another with the railroad industry, the town's newspaper offered ample coverage of railroad happenings. As the Katy's William Crush began planning his crash in the late summer of 1896, the Sedalia newspaper kept its readers abreast of the latest developments.

Rag Time Musicale

FOREST PARK

Wednesday Night, June 27, One Night Only.

Scott Joplin and Henry Jackson's "Rag Time Musicale," introducing Scott Joplin's latest composition, "The Rag Time Song and Dance Quadrille," will be given at Forest Park, one night, June 27. This will be the hottest thing of its kind ever given in Sedalia, as the best talent in the city has been secured. Scott Joplin, the author of "The Maple Leaf Rag," is the director, and having had an experience in this line of business for several years, everybody can look for a real rag time reception. Miss Annie Smith, the Black Patti of Missouri, has consented to render some of her most beautiful and enchanting melodies, assisted very ably by the famous warblers of Blackville, "The Sedalia Medley Quartette." ADMISSION, 10 c.

Newspaper ad placed by Scott Joplin for a Rag Time Musicale in Sedalia, Missouri. *Author's collection.*

Clearly, either by reading the newspaper or hearing about it from his pal Jackson, Joplin could not have been unaware of the coming smashup in Texas. Whether he and some or all of his troupe bought excursion tickets to Crush, or whether Jackson managed to get them passes, Joplin likely stood among the thousands of others who witnessed the September 15 event. Another possibility is that his Texas Medley Quartette had been one of the ensembles playing in the bandstands the Katy had constructed at the crash site. However Joplin learned about the Crash at Crush, after it was over he realized it would be a good subject for a musical piece. Working quickly, Joplin got the notes in his head down on paper and then went to see Smith and his younger associate, Fuller.

If the two Temple men shared the almost universal southern racial prejudices of the time—a way of life that ran so deeply that the businessmen could have been scorned for even doing business with a black man—they did not allow that view to affect what was obviously a good business decision. The Katy's staged train wreck had received so much publicity that it logically followed that a piece of sheet music inspired by the crash would sell plenty of copies.

At this point in Joplin's career, mostly only other African Americans knew of and appreciated the extent of his musical talents. Most whites who bought his sheet music would have assumed he was white. Clearly, Smith and Fuller believed that Joplin's composition would appeal to both sides of the figurative tracks. Within weeks of the crash, the Temple music store had the seven-page "Great Crush Collision March" for sale at forty cents per copy. Printed on cream stock, its title stood out in large, fancy red type. Only slightly smaller was the name of its composer, followed in much smaller type by the notation that Joplin was also "Author of 'Harmony Club' Waltz and 'Combination' March." This time, the publisher was listed as Fuller, whose name appeared in large type, with "Robt. Smith, Agent" below Fuller's name in a smaller font. Curiously, perhaps for marketability, the top of the cover of the Crush piece pointed out that the arrangement was "Dedicated to the M.K. & T. Ry." Of most import, at least for Fuller, was that he held the copyright to the work.

Kent Biffle, longtime *Dallas Morning News* columnist, had a theory about how Joplin came to write the Crush march. "Could brash Willie Crush have bought the work by Joplin *before* [Biffle's emphasis] the great crash? I think so." If the composition were a work for hire commissioned by the MKT, that explains why Joplin did not own the copyright. Still, that leaves unanswered how Fuller came by the copyright.

Joplin's biographers dismiss the "Harmony Club Waltz" and "Combination March" as workmanlike if unremarkable compositions, but they say the Crush piece foreshadowed the musical greatness that was soon to come.

Though called a march, the Crush composition is more accurately a descriptive overture, similar to later works by E.T. Paull, who had already done a piece called "Chariot Race or Ben Hur March." Authors Rudi Blesh and Harriet Janis in their book *They All Played Ragtime* described the Crush piece as having:

> *A bombastic opening of descending octaves* [that] *leads to three separate sixteen-measure themes, the last a trio, and each repeated. These are followed by a long section of thirty-two bars, consisting of two separate themes. As heavy treble chords played over a rapid running chromatic bass,*

the printed, between-the-lines description reads: "The noise of the trains while running at the rate of sixty miles per hour." Then: "Whistling for the crossing," with four-note treble discords, two long and two short; then "The train noise," followed once more by "Whistle before the collision," conveyed by four short, frantic discords higher up. Then comes "The collision," a heavy low double forte chord on the diminished seventh.

As researcher Terri Jo Ryan wrote for a website called Waco History, "This approach brings to mind the kind of scoring that would become standard for Hollywood pictures in the decades following [the march's] publication. It was an attempt to insert narrative flair into what was otherwise a fairly straightforward composition and was a foreshadowing of Joplin's later work with dramatic compositions."

Some music scholars believe that while the Crush piece was marketed as a march, it contains syncopation that could easily be played as ragtime. While no original recording of Joplin playing the march exists to prove it, they believe its author did eventually play the piece, or at least a part of it, in ragtime.

How much money the Crush march made for its composer and the copyright owner is not known, but musical historians see the crash-based score as a milepost indicating that Joplin's technical skill was picking up speed and moving on down the line toward national recognition. His march was still selling sixteen months after the crash, the *New Orleans Times-Picayune* noting on February 27, 1898, in a short listing headlined "New Music" that it had received from L. Grunewald Company a copy of Joplin's "Great Crush Collision March" sheet music.

At that time, Joplin was still in Sedalia, where in 1897 he had enrolled at George R. Smith College for Negroes, studying piano and music. Two years later, inspired by his frequent gigs at Sedalia's Maple Leaf Club, the Texas-born musician composed what would become his classic work, "Maple Leaf Rag."

In the summer of 1900, Joplin and Henry Jackson (whether he was still an MKT porter is not known) promoted a "Rag Time Musicale" in Sedalia's Forest Park. At the June 27 event, Joplin debuted his latest composition, "The Rag Time Song and Dance Quadrille." He and his fellow members of the Texas Medley Quartette paid for a large ad that ran in the *Sedalia Democrat* on four consecutive days prior to the event. "This will be the hottest thing of its kind ever given in Sedalia," the ad promised, "as the best talent in the city has been secured." Obviously written by

Joplin, the ad assured the public that all who attended could "look for a real rag time reception."

Only four and a half years after the spectacle at Crush, the *Sedalia Democrat* published on March 8, 1901, a substantial article on Joplin. "The Ragtime King" the top line of a four-deck headline declared. While making no mention of Joplin's Crush-inspired composition, the newspaper quoted Alfred Ernst, director of the St. Louis Symphony, as saying that Joplin had a bright future. The article did note in the first paragraph that Joplin was black, but the overall tone was positive for the Jim Crow era.

"The work Joplin has done in ragtime is so original, so distinctly individual, and so melodious withal, that I am led to believe he can do something fine in compositions of a higher class when he shall have been instructed in theory and harmony," Ernst declared.

That said, the director plainly did not think much of ragtime as a musical form. "Joplin's work, as yet," he continued, "has a certain crudeness, due to his lack of musical education, but it shows that the soul of the composer is there and needs but to be set free by knowledge of technique. He is an unusually intelligent young man and fairly well educated."

Ernst wanted to take Joplin to Germany to turn him into a classicist, but that never happened. With the "Maple Leaf Rag" and like tunes, Joplin had not only found his niche, he had pioneered a new type of distinctly American music that led to further innovations.

In 1907, his "Great Crush Collision March" largely forgotten, Joplin moved from Missouri to New York City's Tin Pan Alley. By the time of his death on April 1, 1917, from complications related to syphilis, he had composed some sixty works.

It is well documented that Joplin shared with friends his belief that he would never achieve true critical acclaim in his lifetime, and that is what happened. Sixty-five years in his grave, he was rediscovered in 1973 when his 1902 ragtime piece "The Entertainer" was adapted for use as the theme for the hit 1973 film *The Sting*. In March 1974, the score won an Academy Award.

Two years later, Joplin received a second posthumous honor. In 1911, he had published an opera, *Treemonisha*, set near Texarkana that had other obvious autobiographical elements as well. The protagonist is Treemonisha, the adopted daughter of former slaves Ned and Monisha. Her parents found her under a tree when she was a baby, hence her unusual name. Like Joplin, her life was changed by a white person who saw to her education. This is the Library of Congress's summary of the work:

Like many creative types, musician Scott Joplin's greatest recognition came years after his death with a posthumous Pulitzer Prize and a U.S. postage stamp issued in his honor. *Author's collection.*

Treemonisha deals with the conflicts in African-American culture at the end of the 19th century—the desire to move into mainstream American society countered by the strange pull of the old African ways and superstitions. Treemonisha is kidnapped by the so-called "conjure men," but is rescued and returned home, where she becomes a leader among her community. The theme of the work—the importance of an education for both men and women—is powerfully set against music that borrows all of the elements of European opera and merges them with the unique rhythms of ragtime.

Never produced in his lifetime but finally staged for the first time in 1972, four years later the opera earned Joplin a posthumous Pulitzer Prize.

THE SHOW GOES ON...AND ON

A few days after the deadly spectacle at Crush, an editorial writer for the *St. Louis Republic* in effect said that when it came to staging train wrecks for profit, enough was enough. "No More of These Fakes," the *Sedalia Democrat* agreed in commenting on the *Republic*'s stand. "The fatalities attending the M.K. & T.'s collision exhibition near Waco, Tex., will probably put an end to that form of spectacular amusement," the Kansas article said. The piece went on:

> *It is perhaps just as well that this character of exhibition be abandoned. No practical benefit was ever subserved thereby, beyond making cast-off motive power and dilapidated rolling stock serve as revenue producers. From a scientific standpoint these spectacles have had no value, and have added nothing to the sum of mechanical knowledge. They have not pointed out any way of avoiding collisions of railroad trains nor of mitigating their security when they do occur. The practical results are nil, and the risk of human destruction is too great to justify further experiment in the same direction.*

While few reasonable people could argue with that view, the editorial writer obviously misunderstood human nature. Who could resist what likely would be a once-in-a-lifetime chance to see a spectacular train wreck firsthand? More importantly, as the St. Louis newspaper had pointed out, such events would "serve as revenue producers" for anyone with the organizational and promotional skills to stage them.

Even as the presses rolled in St. Louis and Sedalia and at other newspapers opposed to such dangerous events, a thirty-eight-year-old farmer and auctioneer named Joe S. Connolly completed his plans for a locomotive smashup near Merriam, Kansas, on the outskirts of Kansas City. Set for October 6, the crash would be a thrilling new addition to the annual Kansas City Karnival Krewe. Soon to become nationally known as "Head-On" Joe, Connolly had embarked on a new career as a professional train wreck producer.

The myth would arise that the Crash at Crush is what inspired Connolly to get into the train crashing business, but it is clear that Streeter's exhibition in Ohio on Memorial Day 1896 is what motivated Connolly—that and having watched trains of the Chicago & Northwestern Railway pass by his family's farm house when he was a kid and wondering what it would be like if two locomotives were to hit each other pilot-to-pilot. Some writers have said that Connolly had come to Texas to see the Katy crash, but there is no known evidence of that and it seems highly unlikely.

One of the seventy-three locomotive crashes staged by Iowa promoter "Head-On" Joe Connolly. This was a collision he orchestrated at the 1902 Wisconsin State Fair. *Author's collection.*

Two Engines Smash Head-On at State Fair

ON SATURDAY, SEPTEMBER 3, ONE DAY ONLY, two gigantic railroad locomotives, driven straight at each other at terrific speed, will crash head-on in front of the Grandstand at the Minnesota State Fair. It will be the most thrilling attraction on the program of the big Exposition, September 3 to 10.

A straight track, one-half mile long, has been laid inside of the mile track at the State Fair. One engine has been placed at the east end of the track, another engine has been placed at the west end.

At the appointed time on the afternoon program, the two monsters of the rails, shaking under a terrific head of steam, will be turned loose. The throttles will be thrown wide open, and the engineers and firemen will jump for their lives. Traveling at tremendous speed the two locomotives will crash head-on in front of the grandstand, two rods north of the half-mile track.

Railroad collisions of this sort have been staged as a sole attraction in different parts of the country and have attracted 150,000 persons at one time. The Railroad Collision Saturday will be only one feature on a heavy entertainment bill. There will be horse racing, auto polo, music, vaudeville, and the passage of Daredevil James from auto to aeroplane. In the evening there will be a mammoth fireworks spectacle.

It is no wonder that the Minnesota State Fair has become generally known as the World's Greatest State Fair. It is no wonder that the Northwest has grown to appreciate it so much as to practically double its attendance in five years. We have spent hundreds of thousands of dollars on your program this year. We seek your co-operation. Let's see you at the Collision.

Large newspaper ad touting at "Head-On" Joe train crash at the 1921 Minnesota State Fair. *Author's collection.*

In fact, on June 4, only a few days after the first-ever crash near Columbus, Connolly pitched the idea of a staged train wreck to the Iowa State Agricultural Society, the entity that ran the Iowa State Fair at Des Moines. The minutes of that meeting reflect that Connolly made a proposal to crash two trains together at forty miles an hour in front of the fair's grandstand. He could do it for $5,000, he said. The board said no thanks.

The tall, red-headed, quiet-spoken Iowan apparently did not like hearing the word *no*. The following month, on July 10, he was back before the board with an amended proposal. This time, he said he could pull off a locomotive smashup for $3,000. Clearly, Connolly did not lack self-confidence. Predicting that scheduling such an event would double the best gate ever on the fair's best-ever Thursday, and double the amount taken in on the best day ever at the fair's amphitheater, he told the board he would take as the balance of his fee anything over that amount. This time the board took the matter under advisement.

The next time Connolly appeared before the board, he bent to its request for a bigger cut of the take, and the members voted to allow him to proceed. He did so with the help of J.H. Bancroft, a longtime engineer with the Chicago & Northwestern Railroad. It is unclear whether he was in partnership with Connolly or represented the railroad. Since tracks had to be laid to accommodate the trains and the junker locomotives cost more than Connolly could have afforded, it seems probable that the railroad was taking part in the event for the publicity. That, or the confident young Iowan had agreed to pay the railroad from his gross.

Whatever their private arrangement, in the press Bancroft made it sound like the whole thing was his and that he would be running the show. But instead of obtaining expendable rolling stock from the Chicago & Northwestern, Connolly got the Des Moines, Northern & Western Railroad to provide him with two obsolete sixty-ton locomotives, to be paid for out of the gate. Then he and Bancroft started a vigorous promotional campaign that paid off. On the day of the event, an estimated fifty to seventy thousand people showed up and ticket receipts reportedly exceeded $10,000.

Among those on hand, but not solely for the show, were two attorneys. One was Connolly's brother and the other an attorney representing Bancroft. The meeting of the two lawyers proved almost as loud as the coming train collision would be—assuming it would happen.

Everything was ready to go, but a problem arose. As the spectators looked on, Connolly and his brother; Bancroft and his lawyer; and Fred Hubbard, who had sold the well-used locomotives to Connolly, engaged in a heated discussion while standing between the two soon-to-be-demolished engines, excess steam escaping from the locomotive's respective valves. Hubbard wanted his money up front or the deal was off, he said. But when fair officials refused to hand over any cash to Connolly before the exhibition, all parties involved finally agreed to settle up after the event.

Finally, at 5:00 p.m., Bancroft signaled for the trains to start moving. As the engineer in each opposing train pulled the throttle back, the two locomotives began their final run. Before they picked up too much speed, the crew jumped out and ran to distance themselves from the eminent collision.

"There was a smashing of iron, hissing of steam from the broken boilers and fall apart of the old engines, which mingling together, fell in a heap," the *Des Moines Daily News* reported. And as had been the case at the earlier crashes, scores of spectators surged forward to collect souvenirs from the wreckage.

The crowd obviously considered the event a literal smashing success. Fair records show Connolly made $3,538 on the deal, while Bancroft netted $2,000.

Whether Connolly ever worked again with Bancroft is not known, but the staged wreck in his home state set Connolly on a lifelong career track. Of course, Connolly had no franchise. Nine days after the event in Des Moines, another promoter staged the crashing together of two narrow-gauge steam engines at the city fair in Sioux City, Iowa.

More than six hundred miles away, on the last day of September 1896 in Denver, the local Democratic Party staged a fundraising head-ender with two aged narrow-gauge locomotives furnished by the Union Pacific, Denver & Gulf Railroad. Taking a jab at the opposing party, one of the about-to-be-demolished locomotives was named "McKinley" and the other "Hanna," for Republican National Committee chairman Mark Hanna. Net proceeds from the crash presumably went to support Democratic candidates.

Connolly, meanwhile, successfully conducted his second demolition derby in Kansas. Continuing the shtick developed by Alfred Streeter, Connolly named the opposing locomotives "Gold Standard" and "Free Silver." Some twenty thousand people paid to see the train wreck, but the two locomotives closed on each other at only fifteen miles an hour and the crowd left somewhat disappointed.

Although he only had a role in a few pay-to-see crashes in 1896, Connolly realized that staged train wrecks just might be his ticket to wealth. Failing that, the train wrecking business could at least earn him a living. Still, he proceeded modestly, gaining momentum—and a reputation—as the years passed. Hedging his bet early on, he continued his ownership of a movie house in Des Moines, although he leased it to another party. In 1907, his peak year for events, he oversaw six crashes. He did one in Milwaukee; one in Oklahoma City; one in St. Joseph, Missouri; and one at Brighton Beach in Brooklyn, New York. He also put to the lie any future claims that the Crash at Crush was the only such event in Texas history. Connolly executed well-attended crashes in Fort Worth and San Antonio that year.

In fact, San Antonio has a claim to fame hardly anyone knows about. It saw more staged train crashes than any other city in the United States. The Alamo City crashes, all coordinated by Connolly, occurred in 1904, 1905, 1907 and 1908. All of the shows were part of the San Antonio International Fair, an annual exhibition and livestock event begun in 1888 that for a time rivaled Dallas's State Fair of Texas in attendance.

Planning the 1905 International Fair crash presented the Iowa promoter a novel challenge. Unusual as it was to get a chance to witness a train wreck, something even more unusual was in the air, quite literally. Professor Carl E. Meyers of Frankfort, New York, would be ascending in one his hydrogen-filled balloon airships. Connolly wanted no competition with something as novel as one of the professor's flying machines, as balloons with motors were called before "flying machine" became synonymous with "airplane" for a time. Accordingly, "Head-On" Joe struck a deal with Meyers: the professor agreed to make his flight in the morning so Connolly could crash his locomotives in the afternoon.

The MKT also had some involvement in the Alamo City smashup that year in that it handled the delivery of the two sacrificial locomotives from St. Louis to San Antonio. In addition, the Katy had a large-scale model of its Flyer on display at the fair. Whether Crush had any dealings with Connolly or came down from Dallas to take in the show is not known, but newspaper accounts note that numerous members of the Texas legislature were on hand along with the two men running for governor.

The 25,973 people who bought tickets to see the crash did not go away disappointed. Racing toward each other from opposite ends of 3,200 feet of track, the two ninety-ton locomotives smashed together spectacularly. Once souvenir hunters had hauled off all the pieces they could, Connolly sold the wreckage to a salvage dealer for $400. However, that was nothing compared with what he charged the fair association to put on the show: $10,000.

Back in San Antonio in 1907, wanting to offer spectators more bang for their buck (actually, fifty cents), Connolly experimented with what he called "lapped track principle." The rails were put down in such a way that the two engines would scrape against each other's side at high speed before derailing in a dramatic way. It didn't work quite the way he intended, but when one locomotive T-boned the other, the crowd was pleased. After that, Connolly stuck with his generally reliable head-to-head model. He did often use gasoline to ensure a good fire after a collision.

Connolly always strove to put on a good show, but ever mindful of what had happened at Crush, he was a stickler for safety. He had several personal close calls, but with careful planning (which included rigid enforcement of safety zones), trial runs, using experienced engineers and just plain good luck, none of his train wrecks ever resulted in death or injury.

Even other promoters' or organizations' collisions, usually one-off events and often duds compared to a Connolly crash, managed to smash trains without hurting any customers. Not that there weren't some near disasters. On July 4, 1904, multiple thousands of people gathered to see a train smashup arranged by hotelier William H. O'Neill at a resort on the Massachusetts coast called Point of Pines. What began as an attempt among many in the crowd to see the crash for free devolved into a riot that ended with some of the spectators trying to run the locomotives into each other themselves. Police finally dispersed the mob, but not before considerable property damage had occurred. The event was O'Neill's first and last try at train crashing.

Despite one flop in Los Angeles in 1906, promoters on the West Coast were more successful. Train crashes at the California State Fair in 1913–14 and in 1916–17 attracted good crowds, made money and went off as planned. A bonus at the 1917 affair had silent movie star Helen Holmes riding on atop one of the speeding locomotives, only to jump onto a racing automobile at the last moment. After the end of World War I, the crash of two used Santa Fe Railroad locomotives at a fair in Fresno in the fall of 1919 delighted thirty-five thousand spectators.

Twenty-five years into his train wrecking career, Connolly hoped to capitalize on his expertise by marketing a book on how to make money off staging train wrecks. He filed for a copyright in 1921 for a book called *Railway Train and Locomotive Head On Collision for Novelty Exhibition* and registered a related title in 1923 and a third in 1927. But James J. Reisdorff, author of a booklet on Connolly, could not find the books at the Library of Congress (which requires two copies of any copyrighted work) or anywhere else. Connolly also may have tried to patent his system, but if he did, he was not successful.

Above: "Head-On" Joe engineered this crash at the California State Fair. *Author's collection.*

Opposite: Ad from the *Miami News* advancing "The Spectacle of the Century" set for February 23, 1931, one of the last prearranged collisions as the fad faded during the Great Depression. *Author's collection.*

By 1932, "Head-On" Joe had been wrecking trains for the public's fun and his profit for thirty-six years. Now seventy-four, since staging his first train wreck at the Iowa State Fair, Connolly had seen automobiles and airplanes become commonplace, wireless telegraphy had evolved into commercial radio and silent films had been talking for five years. The railroads were even beginning to phase out steam engines in favor of diesel-powered locomotives.

Connolly had begun his unusual business enterprise shortly after the financial depression of the mid-1890s. Now, the nation was in the throes of an even more dire depression. Taking into consideration his age and the times, he figured it was time to retire—but not before one last train wreck. To bring his career full circle, Connolly decided to stage his final crash back where he started—at the Iowa State Fair.

Hoping to offer the citizens of their state some diversion from their troubles, fair officials were planning quite a show. There would be a battery of thrilling exhibitions, from what they called automobile polo to a high-wire act by noted acrobat Cecil Florence. The pièce de résistance, as it had been so many years before, would be the crash of two speeding locomotives.

Connolly signed a contract to do his thing at the fair on August 27, 1932. He procured two steam engines from the Milwaukee Railroad and

Sponsored by Miami Junior Chamber of Commerce Summer Tourist Committee—Direction of American Amusement Company, New York

supervised the laying of three thousand feet of track on the fairgrounds. Having learned his trade well, he had earth mounded so that the opposing trains would get an extra boost from starting on a downhill grade.

In keeping with the tradition begun in Ohio by Alfred Streeter so many years before, each locomotive got a fitting name. Democrat Franklin D. Roosevelt was running against the incumbent, Republican president Herbert Hoover. The election would not be until November 8 that year, but before then, a locomotive labeled "Roosevelt" would meet a locomotive named "Hoover." In this contest, however, neither opponent would emerge as a winner.

Unfortunately for fair planners, it seriously rained on their figurative parade on the Saturday of the scheduled crash. Fortunately, while most of the other acts had to be canceled, the experienced showman was good to go with his swan-song crash, rain or shine. With the face-off of the iron monsters set for 4:00 p.m., the fair's grandstand had been sold out since 1:00 p.m. That amounted to 15,107 people willing to pay fifty cents (which could have bought a hungry family one quart of peanut butter and three loaves of bread with three cents change) to see the crash. An additional 13,301 standing room–only tickets were sold, bringing the total crowd to 28,408.

"At the top of their speed [roughly fifty miles an hour]," the *Des Moines Register* reported the next day, "the engines crashed with a roar, the boiler on the 'Hoover' blew up, hurling out metal for yards, while the cab of the 'Roosevelt' was crashed like an eggshell as the force of the impact telescoped the eastbound locomotive."

Years later, someone who had been there that day said he remembered looking at Connolly for a few seconds when the trains met. The veteran promoter's face was expressionless.

"Well, that's that," he said. Then he walked away.

Epilogue
END OF THE LINE

All trains, and the people who run them or ride on them, sooner or later come to the end of the line. Here's what became of the individuals and institutions involved one way or the other in the Crash at Crush or the national fad of made-to-order locomotive collisions that held sway from the mid-1890s into the 1930s.

ALFRED STREETER

Aristotle observed that there is "no great genius without some touch of madness." Whether Alfred Streeter was gifted or merely bright is unknowable now, but he clearly was an innovative thinker. One thing is certain: he spent his last years in a mental hospital.

After giving up on the locomotive-crashing business, he focused his ample creative energy on the opposite of what he had been doing. He went from smashing trains head-on to perfecting more efficient ways of bringing them to a controlled stop. In that endeavor he succeeded in making a fortune for the times. Even during the financial downturn of 1906, Chicago newspapers called him a millionaire. And that was when coffee cost about thirty-five cents per pound, sirloin steak went for twelve cents per pound and a lady could buy a fine wool suit for nineteen dollars on the high end.

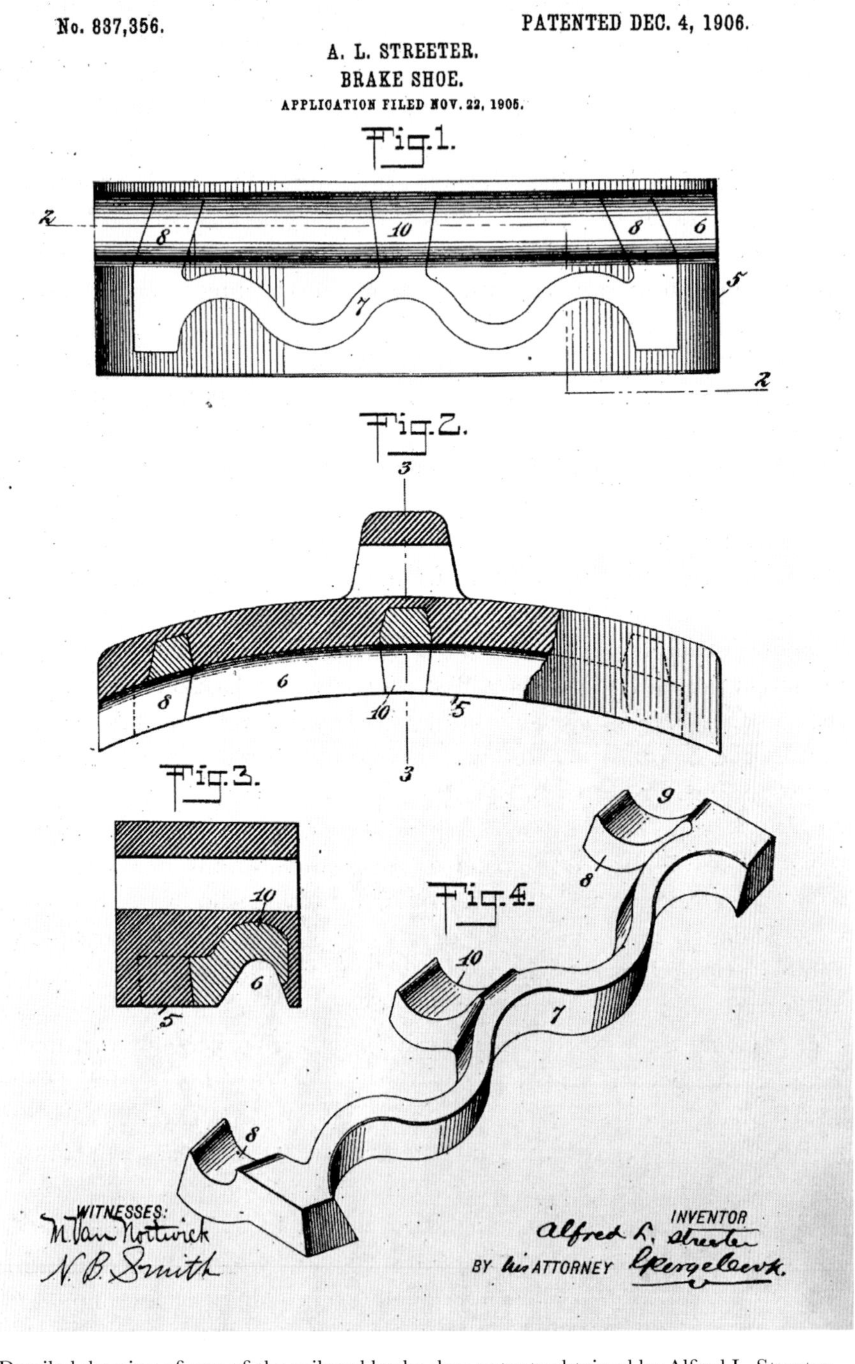

No. 837,356.

PATENTED DEC. 4, 1906.

A. L. STREETER.
BRAKE SHOE.
APPLICATION FILED NOV. 22, 1905.

Fig.1.

Fig.2.

Fig.3.

Fig.4.

WITNESSES:
M. Van Nortwick
N. B. Smith

INVENTOR
Alfred L. Streeter
BY his ATTORNEY George Clark.

Detailed drawing of one of the railroad brake shoe patents obtained by Alfred L. Streeter, whose innovative nature made him a millionaire. *Author's collection.*

Of particular importance to Streeter's success was his common-law wife, Vivian, whom he took up with in 1895, in New Orleans when she was seventeen. A smart southern belle who liked horseback riding, hunting and fishing, she was described by one Chicago newspaper as having been "one of the most beautiful and attractive members of the younger set in New Orleans." She held herself out as Mrs. Alfred Streeter, but she was no stereotypical housewife content to stay home and raise a family.

To help him with his inventions, she took a correspondence course in engineering. An increasingly active partner in his career, "she became so proficient her husband entrusted to her most of the detail work in the experimental work of his inventions." According to the *Chicago Tribune*, "She also gave him several original suggestions that are said by friends to have resulted in great profit."

In 1897, Streeter received a patent for an improved railroad brake shoe he had invented—apparently with help from Vivian. He would go on to obtain a dozen additional patents, all involving some aspect of brake shoes. In early 1900, with two partners and $50,000 in capital, he incorporated the Streeter Brake Shoe Company and began manufacturing and selling his products.

Before long, business being good, he had offices on the thirteenth floor of the seventeen-story Monadnock Building at 53 West Jackson Street, lived in style at the elegant Grace Hotel at 75 West Jackson and had a hunting lodge at Fox Lake, a popular resort town fifty-four miles northwest of Chicago.

Vivian Oliver Streeter believed that she and Alfred shared a wonderful life. Unknown to her was that her special someone happened to be married to two other women: a woman in Cleveland, Ohio, with whom Streeter had a fifteen-year-old son and a woman in Michigan with whom he had an eight-year-old daughter. At one point, police learned, he had been married to yet another woman, but she had since died. Whether he had merely forgotten to divorce those women before taking up with Vivian or whether he had been juggling three women at the same time would become a matter of legal dispute. Beyond his multiple wives, since the summer of 1905 he had been keeping a seventeen-year-old girl as his mistress. Even so, everyone apparently got along just fine until one night in August 1906, when Chicago police happened to raid the notorious Renau Hotel on Wabash Avenue.

One of the residents taken into custody was strikingly pretty Hazel Burkle, a young lady from Green Lake, Wisconsin, described by the press as having a "kittenish, saucy face." Letters police found in her room, which was paid for by Streeter, linked her romantically to the wealthy manufacturer. Not only had he been covering her rent, but he had also been paying for her piano

GIRL WITNESS IN HOTEL CASES, BROUGHT TO CHICAGO BY POLICE, AND HER CAPTOR.

Margaret Burkle

One of the residents taken into custody was strikingly pretty Hazel Burkle, a young lady from Green Lake, Wisconsin, described by the press as having a "kittenish, saucy face." While this image identifies her as "Margaret," she went by "Hazel." *Author's collection.*

and dancing lessons and buying her fine dresses. As one of the Chicago newspapers soon put it, the teenager had been "transformed from a happy, virtuous girl to a girl who didn't care."

Soon indicted for "harboring a girl under age" (essentially statutory rape) and likely facing another indictment for bigamy, Streeter decided that it would be a great time to visit Canada. From St. Thomas, Ontario—safe from extradition and the wrath of the wronged women in his life—he directed his business interests and possibly tried to explain things to Vivian, his wives and his mistress by mail.

Meanwhile, to the delight of the Chicago newspapers, the scandal grew. The father of Streeter's teenage mistress threatened to shoot the forty-five-year-old industrialist on sight, as did her six older brothers. Then the girl disappeared from the juvenile girls' home. When authorities found her, she tried to commit suicide. Prosecutors and police were now looking at a possible conspiracy case against Streeter, his attorney and others in connection with the girl's mysterious "escape." Then, on December 1, fifty-nine-year-old David F. Jennings, one of Streeter's closest business associates, stood in front of a lavatory mirror adjacent to their offices, put a revolver to his temple and pulled the trigger.

Streeter stayed gone three years. Finally, in the fall of 1908, his lawyer succeeded in getting the indictment quashed. Although he escaped any criminal consequences, Vivian left him and soon married patent medicine millionaire Frank J. Kellogg in Michigan. Chicago newspapers are silent on how Streeter's wives took the news that the father of their children had been living with another woman in Illinois and seeing an underage girl on the side, but it likely had a chilling effect on their relationships.

The kicker is that Vivian, later divorcing Kellogg, would admit in a state court that she had never actually been legally married to Streeter, even though they had lived together as man and wife for six years. Of course, no one but she and Streeter knew that at the time of the Chicago scandal.

In 1916, the year he obtained his last brake shoe patent, a Chicago newspaper reported that Streeter had suffered several paralytic strokes. Four years later, he was a patient at the Chicago State Hospital for the Insane. There he spent the last six years of his life as an inmate (that's the term the U.S. Census for 1920 used). Streeter died at Forest Park, Illinois on August 31, 1926, and was buried at Forest Home Cemetery.

WILLIAM G. CRUSH

Unlike those killed in the aftermath of his disastrous PR stunt, William Crush enjoyed a long and prosperous life. If the deaths that followed the locomotive crash he stage-managed haunted him in later years, no evidence of it has been found.

Unquestionably a company man of the first order, it's safe to assume that he had long since rationalized the deaths in McLennan County as tragic accidents associated with unforeseen boiler explosions and carelessness on the part of the victims. A devout Catholic, he also may have found solace in confession and absolution.

The story has persisted that he was fired on the spot after the boilers exploded and railroad officials realized that fatalities and injuries had resulted. The punch line to that oft-told story is that once the powers that be with Katy understood how much generally favorable publicity the line had received, Crush was rehired about a week after the collision. That makes for a good read, but more than likely he kept his job without interruption.

In recalling the event in 1957, surviving participant Frank Barnes said, "Crush was not blamed for the explosion." Crush's hometown newspaper, the *Dallas Morning News*, noted in a 1903 article about him, "The unfortunate explosion which was caused by the collision was not in any way his fault and could not have been foreseen." Another argument against the likelihood of his firing is that as the man in charge, he had to oversee the evacuation of the injured spectators and the departure of the excursion trains and tend to all the other loose ends.

Whatever the truth, Crush spent the rest of his working life with the Katy in ever-more responsible positions until late in his career, when the railroad's management finally hoisted him off the fast track and gave him lighter duties in anticipation of the day he would end up "on the shelf," as railroaders called retirement.

Less than a year after the spectacular collision at the short-lived town named in his honor, Crush garnered more publicity for the Katy when his company pioneered a new piece of rolling stock it called the Flying Katy. (It couldn't name it the Katy Flyer because that was what its express passenger train was called.)

The Flying Katy wasn't exactly a train, even if it did roll along the tracks. The company's shop in Sedalia, Kansas, had designed and built a steam-powered version of the traditional human-powered handcar—only this one was fancier.

Here's how one newspaper described it:

> The Flying Katy is equipped with an upright boiler and engine and is capable of making 35 miles an hour if the occasion requires, although the ordinary rate of speed is about 20 miles an hour. It carries a crew of two men, an engineer and fireman. Eight persons can travel in comfort, but on the recent long trip it carried but two. . . . The car is open all around, but is supplied with curtains which can be lowered in case of a storm. Two seats, luxuriously cushioned, extend across the entire front of the car, and this is where the passengers ride. The engineer and fireman occupy places in the rear.

In the summer of 1897, Crush and his boss, general passenger agent James Baker, undertook a three-week inspection tour of the entire Katy system, from St. Louis to Galveston. In doing so, they covered roughly two thousand miles of track.

They stopped at every station on the main line and its branches and took photographs of the company property. The two men collected information on every point on the line, from whistle-stops to Katy's depots in small towns and large cities. That data would be compiled into a report for the company's upper management. "Probably never before was so complete an inspection of railroad property made," a newspaper account of the trip noted.

At every station they hit, the two men, whose job it was to increase passenger traffic on the line, inquired as to what the local population was, whether the community was growing or stagnant, if local farmers anticipated bringing in a good crop that year and "many other questions regarding the conditions of the country."

The congenial Crush did most of the talking at each stop, and he soon adapted a routine system of information-gathering.

"At one station at which the party stopped no town was visible," the newspaper continued. "But Mr. Crush unthinkingly put the usual questions to the station agent. 'What is the population of this town?' 'Three people,' answered the agent, 'myself, wife and baby.'" At another stop, when Crush asked about the population, the station agent said, "Thirty-nine people, I counted myself last week."

Otherwise, the article on the Flying Katy noted, the conveyance only stopped "when one of the passengers wanted to light a cigar or get a drink."

Later that summer, Crush was asked to umpire a fundraising baseball game at the state fair park. Not naming the charity, the *Dallas Morning News* published on August 28, 1897, a fun-poking article about the upcoming event that must have been written by someone who knew the Katy official. While the game itself had generated some excitement, the story said, "the crowning feature and attraction is going to be the umpire."

Game planners had initially been uncertain who should officiate at the game, but after much discussion, "it was finally decided that the man who had succeeded in handling 47 excursion trains, 35,000 people and a head-on collision all at one and the same time…was the only person who could creditably discharge the onerous duties of an umpire." Keeping tongue-in-cheek, the writer added that Crush would be carrying a piston rod from one of the destroyed locomotives for use as a cane and weapon of both defense and offense.

Three years later, the 1900 U.S. Census showed that the Crush family had three live-in domestic servants, a black laborer, a cook and a white Irish housekeeper. Crush was active in the Knights of Columbus, and he and his wife were part of Dallas society. The couple lived well, but Crush continued to be well worth his salary to the Katy's management.

In addition to generating revenue for the company by keeping the line's regularly scheduled passenger runs as full as possible, Crush continued to make money for the Katy through excursion trains—extra trains filled with passengers who paid a special excursion rate. Beyond capitalizing on fairs, political conventions, association meetings, football games and other scheduled events—as Crush had demonstrated with his famous crash—he believed in creating events that would necessitate special trains.

In 1912, Crush pulled off another economic coup for the Katy, one that also netted his employer considerable—and this time totally favorable—publicity. When he learned that the American Association of Advertising Clubs would be having its annual convention in Dallas, Crush went to work to convince the association's leadership that the MKT should be the railroad on which they traveled to Texas.

Economically, the stakes were big. More than eight hundred "ad men," as they were called, would be coming to the Lone Star State, many for the first time. Crush succeeded in getting the association to contract with the Katy to get its delegates from St. Louis to Dallas. "Mr. Crush was complimented on all sides, especially by fellow railroad men, on account of his success in persuading the great bulk of the ad men who will meet in Dallas next month to ride from St. Louis via the Katy," the *Houston Post* reported.

Not only would the Katy be getting the ad men to Dallas, but after the convention it would also be taking them on a tour of the state in special trains. "Among the specials will be one from Boston and New England and another from Montreal, Toronto, Ottawa and other cities of Canada," the newspaper continued.

Crush admitted that pulling the deal off had not been without effort. "It needed some hustling to hook 'em," he told the newspaper, "but I am an old fisherman." In addition to all the customers the ad convention would bring to Texas, the old fisherman hoped to lure them back on their own. "We are going to show every visitor and every Texan who makes the tour the time of their lives," Crush promised. "They will see a great portion of Texas during the rarest days of the year [spring] in this state. If half of them don't come back the first opportunity, I'll miss my guess."

Always well spoken, Crush had by this point in his career become the voice of the Katy, at least for newspaper reporters. Of course, like any good spokesman, he knew when to keep his mouth shut. He left the really big announcements for the brass to handle.

Crush continued as general passenger agent for the Katy in Texas until 1918, when the line and all other U.S. railroads fell under federal control during World War I. After the government relinquished its management of the railroads in 1920, Crush soon was named passenger traffic manager for the entire Katy system. That same year, he applied for a U.S. passport, noting that he needed it for business-related travel to Mexico.

When some 1,400 members of six Federated Shop Craft Union locals went on strike in the summer 1922, a union action that resulted in a gubernatorial declaration of martial law in Denison, reporters turned to Crush for the Katy's take on the disruptive and occasionally violent work stoppage. On a more pleasant note, Crush also was generally the one discussing new Katy services, particularly the inauguration of another premier passenger train, the Bluebonnet Special.

Beyond his news-media relations work, tangible results of Crush's contribution to the Katy could only be found in the ledger books. But in the early 1920s, Crush's efforts resulted in a more public monument to his influence in the company.

The longtime Katy executive lived in Dallas's most affluent suburb, Highland Park. In fact, he had been one of the development's first residents when lots first went on sale in 1907. Highland Park, which covered high land overlooking downtown, was the place to live by 1920. Crush correctly believed that his well-to-do neighbors, not to mention the students and faculty of nearby Southern Methodist University, would appreciate having a depot nearer to where they lived than the downtown Union Depot. Many travelers, he argued, did not like the city's Union Station, where they had to climb a lot of steps once they got off a train. Though a member of the Dallas Athletic Club, at fifty-five he may have begun to realize firsthand that stairs were easier for younger folks to climb than people his age or older. As they had for throughout most of his career, upper management agreed with him, and the company invested $37,000 in a small, new depot at the intersection of Euclid and Adams Avenues. The northbound Texas Special stopped there for the first time at 4:10 p.m., July 1, 1922, and the station would continue in use for as long as the Katy ran passenger trains.

Ever frugal, the company installed only one employee at the station, an African American porter the company magazine identified only as "Jake." As Crush had predicted, the station saw a lot of use. In addition to regular traffic, during the fall each year, SMU students and fans crowded the depot to board Katy football specials for out-of-town games.

On October 1, 1930, Crush was promoted to assistant to the vice-president in charge of traffic. That year's federal census gave his net worth as $25,000. An income like that allowed him and his wife to employ a live-in domestic, as well as a chauffeur. The enumerator also noted that they owned a radio. At mid-decade, the railroad gave Crush lighter duty and placed him in charge of the Highland Park station with the title of special passenger representative.

William G. Crush's Highland Park residence in Dallas still stands. *Photo by Rusty Williams.*

MKT payroll records have not survived, but that soft retirement likely came in 1933, his fortieth anniversary with the company. Strong circumstantial evidence is the January 1934 issue of the company magazine, which featured his photograph on its cover. Inside was an article on Crush and his long service that covered a full page and part of another.

In explaining why his portrait graced its cover, the magazine said it was

> *not merely because he has served the Katy so long and faithfully, and has, in so doing, gained for himself and the railroad such a wide circle of friends, but because he originated or helped to develop so many ideas that have done so much to spread the fame and popularity of our railroad, and because he did so much to establish the Katy definitely in the mind of the public, as a progressive and up to date and friendly carrier.*

The article spoke of his winning personality, ready wit and hospitality. He had energy and daring tempered by "keen judgment." But in doing his work, he had a strong sense of ethics and played by the rules. One thing the article didn't mention was the 1896 Crash at Crush. It did, however, note that his "flair for advertising was his most conspicuous attribute in the days of his greatest activity."

In 1935, *Dallas Times-Herald* editor-in-chief Tom Gooch, who had been with the afternoon newspaper since 1901 and doubtless had known Crush a long time, wrote that the Katy executive and three other prominent Dallas men "have never, to our certain knowledge, looped-the-loop or negotiated a spiral glide" in an airplane. But all four men, he said, "did their part in giving aviation a good push forward" in their

Late in his career, William G. Crush made the cover of the *MKT Employee Magazine. Author's collection.*

city. Obviously, Crush did his long-distance travel as he always had, by rail, preferably on one of his line's deluxe trains like the Texas Special. That he was a pioneer in Dallas's evolution as a major air hub is a curiosity Gooch did not explore.

Finally, fifty-four years after he first went to work for the Katy, Crush retired fully in 1940. He was seventy-four years old. Counting his prior service with the Monon Route in Louisville and Chicago, he had been a railroad man for fifty-seven years. A brief item in the August 1940 issue of the in-house magazine noted that he had been under treatment for an unspecified illness at Dallas's St. Paul Hospital. In its October 1940 issue, the magazine reported that Crush was back home.

Even in retirement, Crush could not let go of the Katy. He made it his business to be at the Highland Park station every day to watch the passenger trains come and go, greeting people he knew and smiling at those he didn't. Of course, most of those passing through the suburban depot had no idea that he was the one who had gotten the station built.

Other than family and friends, the railroad was his life. Until the Katy constructed a seven-story headquarters building in downtown Dallas in 1912, his office had been at the old red brick MKT Depot at Lamar and Main Streets. There he had toiled at a desk, not on the trains or in the yards, but his job and everyone else's in the railroad business centered on

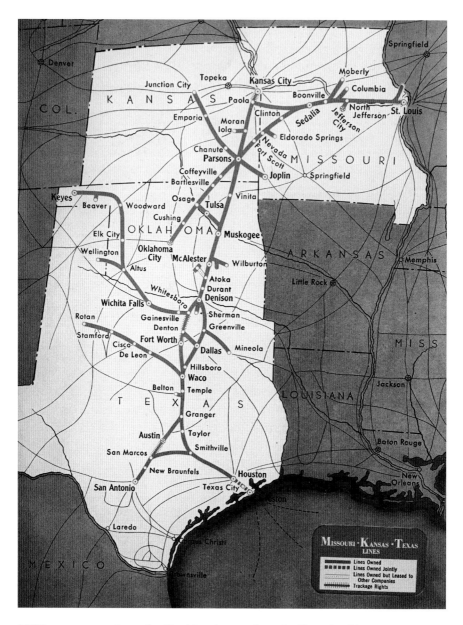

MKT route map not long after Crush's retirement from the Katy after fifty-seven years as a railroad man. *Author's collection.*

one thing: the daily arrivals and departures of passenger and freight trains. He had never tired of the symphony of sounds a locomotive made, the pulsating release of steam that seemed almost like breathing, the spinning driver wheels and slack-jerks when it began to move, the longs and the shorts of its whistle, the clanging of its bell, the whoosh of air brakes engaging or releasing or the screech of metal on metal.

Still, as old men do, he thought about his and the Katy's glory years—the fast, luxurious passenger trains like the Katy Flyer and the Bluebonnet Special and all the things he had done to keep their coaches full. He was proud of the fact that in promoting special events and developing new business for the line, he and the Katy had played a significant role in the growth and prosperity of the states his company served.

But everything was changing, as everything always had and always would. He knew that the Katy had last purchased steam locomotives in 1925, and after the world war ended, the company would be scraping them for diesel power.

Katy general passenger agent Crush was instrumental in getting his company to construct the Highland Park Station in Dallas. The suburban depot was razed in 1965 not long after the MKT ended its passenger service. *Author's collection.*

Crush reached his final destination on April 12, 1943, dying of heart and renal issues at his residence in Highland Park. Three days later, he was buried at Dallas's Calvary Hill Cemetery. His widow lived a few years longer, dying in 1945. The couple never had children. The Associated Press moved a five-paragraph story on Crush's death, devoting the last three of those paragraphs to the spectacular locomotive crash he had staged forty-six years earlier, one of the more remarkable events in the history of American railroading.

The Engineers

Charles Cain

Thirty-six when he jumped from the locomotive Number 1001 at Crush, longtime Katy engineer Charles Cain had a lot riding on not being injured: his wife was pregnant with their second child, born two months after the crash.

Originally from Iowa, where he was born on June 16, 1860, Cain came to Texas at some point prior to 1887, when records show he was working for the Katy in Denison. He married Amanda J. McBride in Williamson County, Texas, on November 25, 1891.

The Cains lived in Smithville, Texas, a Katy division point, and Cain continued to operate out of the yard there until 1916, when he and his wife moved to San Antonio. When he died there of a stroke in March 1925, he had been a Katy employee for nearly forty years.

Cain's brief obituary in the *San Antonio Express* made no mention of his involvement in the Crash at Crush. The article did note that his body would be taken to Smithville for burial, but the location of his grave has not been determined.

Charles E. Stanton

Like many locomotive engineers, Charles Ezra Stanton—the man who had been chosen to take engine Number 999 on its last run—had started out as a railroad fireman. When he came to Texas is not known, but by 1887, he was listed in the Denison City Directory as a fireman for the MKT. He lived in a boardinghouse.

Born on March 12, 1866, at Swanton Swan, Vermont, Stanton was married to Jennie Daisy Stanton (her father's name happened to be Stanton) on October 16, 1895, in St. Paul, Minnesota. The couple never had children.

Stanton and his wife were living in Smithville when he was selected to run Number 999, and he continued working out of that busy Katy yard until 1910. By then, he was listed as a "traveling" engineer. That kept the couple moving around a lot, but by 1917, they were living in Waco, where he was then an inspector for the MKT. Three years later, he and his wife moved to Dallas following his promotion to chief locomotive inspector. They remained in Dallas until sometime prior to 1940, when census records show the Stantons were back in Waco. At seventy-four, he was still on the Katy payroll.

In December 1947, by then four years a widower, Stanton went to St. Paul to help his brother-in-law move to Arizona. On that trip, he suffered a serious stroke but remained alert for a few days before dying on December 28. During that time, according to his obituary in the Waco newspaper, he was able to write a farewell letter to one of his old railroad friends. He left his estate of $25,000 to be divided among his brother-in-law (who was to receive $150 per month for the rest of his life), two old railroad buddies and an orphan's home. He was buried beside his wife in Fond du Lac, Wisconsin.

The headline over his obituary read, "Wacoan Who Aided in Famous Train Crash Stunt Dies."

The Firemen

Frank Barnes

Of all those involved in the Crash at Crush, Barnes—who rode on Number 999—was the only one who wrote in any detail about his experience. He was interviewed for the Katy employee magazine in 1950 and then went on to write a first-person story that was published in *True West* magazine in 1957.

His life story began in Lynn, Indiana, where he was born on December 4, 1871. The family moved to Lone Tree, Nebraska, at some point before 1880. By the time of the 1890 census, the family had relocated to Texas, where they lived in the Palestine area in Anderson County. In 1892, Barnes joined the MKT as an engine watcher three days before his twenty-first birthday. He soon became a fireman and by 1898 had worked his way up to engineer. It is unclear whether he was living in Denison or Smithville at the time of the crash, although by 1900 he was newly married and living in Smithville.

After the deadly and devastating hurricane of September 8, 1900, hit Galveston, once the railway bridge across the bay had been repaired, Barnes ran the first train to reach the battered island city. Three years later, he moved from operating freight trains to passenger service.

He made his final job-related move, to San Antonio, in 1918. The veteran trainman stuck with steam engines his entire career. "The diesels don't make enough noise and they ride too easy," he told an interviewer. "You don't even know you're on an engine." By 1950, with fifty-eight years of service, Barnes passed his required annual physical and then told his wife he had finally decided to retire. Later asked by a reporter if he thought the Crash at Crush had contributed to science, as William G. Crush had claimed, Barnes quipped, "Well, it proved a lot of people will go a long ways to see a train wreck."

He remained in the Alamo City until moving to Austin, where he was living in 1967 when, at ninety-five, he wrote a final article on his experience at Crush for *Railroad Magazine*. He died in San Antonio at the age of one hundred in October 1971. He was buried in Smithville.

S.M. Dickenson

Seymore M. Dickenson was born in Benton, Illinois, on November 3, 1868. His family moved to Texas at some point after 1880. On June 2, 1887, he married Josie Douglas in Johnson County, Texas.

In the collision at Crush, Dickenson stoked the firebox of Number 1001. By 1900, the U.S. Census showed him living with his wife and three children in Hillsboro, where he worked as a freight man for the MKT. Ten years later, still in Hillsboro, he had risen to engineer. Sometime after 1920, he and his wife had moved to Waco, where he was still an engineer with the Katy.

Dickenson stayed with the MKT until his retirement in 1952. He died three years later in Waco on January 12, 1955, and was buried at Rosemound Cemetery there.

THE BRAKEMEN

Lowery Parsons

Lowery Glenn "Turkey" Parsons, born on June 24, 1862, in Central, South Carolina, during the Civil War, would live for seventy years after he jumped from Number 999 at Crush.

After going to work for the Katy as a brakeman, he lived in Denison. Sometime between 1905 and 1910, he relocated to Hillsboro, another major MKT center. By then he had become a conductor. By 1920, he and his wife, whom he married about the time he moved to Hillsboro, had settled in Smithville, another division point on the Katy.

Parsons continued as a conductor with Katy until his retirement in 1940. He stayed in Smithville, where a considerable number of his retired colleagues lived. He died on June 14, 1966, at the age of 103, the last of the train crew members involved in the Crash at Crush.

Heacock

When interviewed for the *MKT Employee Magazine* in 1950, Frank Barnes said someone he recalled only as "Heacock" had ridden as brakeman on Number 1001. Contemporary newspaper accounts never reported his name.

THE CONDUCTORS

Frank Van Gilder

Frank Evan Van Gilder, conductor for Number 999, was born in Jackson Point, Illinois, in 1860 but spent most of his childhood in Seward City, Nebraska. By the time he was twenty, according to the 1880 census, he was working there as a store clerk. He got into railroad work as a conductor for the Union Pacific. He moved to Missouri at some point before 1888, where he and his wife, Delera, became parents of their first child. Their next child was born in Kansas in 1892. Since Parsons, Kansas, was a division point for the Katy, that may have been where Van Gilder went to work for the railroad. However, he could have joined the MKT earlier when he was in Missouri. When the couple had a son in 1895, the year before the Crash at Crush, they were living in Temple, Texas.

The family's next job-related move was to Houston in 1898, where he was Katy's general yard master and operator of the railroad's lunch counter. He was active as a Shriner and a member of the Switchmen's Union of North America.

Van Gilder left the Katy around the turn of the twentieth century and moved to Stamps, Arkansas, where he was a work train conductor for the Louisiana & Arkansas Railroad. Established in 1887, Stamps was home to the L&A's shops.

But like the doomed train he rode at Crush, Van Gilder soon came to a violent end. On December 1, 1902, he was working as a conductor on a steam shovel train doing maintenance work about a mile south of Spring Hill, Louisiana. Several days before, as one newspaper put it, he had "a personal difficulty" with the train's engineer, J.H. Myers. Conductors had ultimate authority on their train, and after an altercation with Myers in the cab of the locomotive, Van Gilder was trying to throw him off the train when the engineer pulled a pistol and shot him twice. Local authorities called to the scene concluded that Myers had acted in self-defense, and he was not charged in connection with the shooting. As the *Pine Bluff (AR) Daily Graphic* reported the following day, "Both men were well thought of and bore good reputations." Van Gilder's burial place is unknown.

The shooting broke apart his family. By 1905, Van Gilder's two youngest children were living at a Masonic home in Wichita, Kansas.

Thomas H. Webb

Webb was born in Mississippi in August 1860. When he moved to Texas is not known, but he was in Hillsboro, Texas, at the time of the 1900 census and may have been working out of there when he was selected to be on the Number 1001 crew. His brother, Kinchen, lived with him and was listed as a railroad switchman. By 1910, Webb and his wife, Laura, had moved to Smithville, a Katy division point. The couple had one son. Webb was a member of the Order of Railway Conductors and the International Order of Railroad Conductors. The *Houston Post* mentioned in 1913 and 1919 that he was a conductor on the "Waco run." No further information on him past 1919 has been located.

THE PHOTOGRAPHERS

Jervis Deane

After recovering from his injury, "One-Eyed" Deane, as people took to calling him, continued to ply his photography trade in Waco for several years.

He was still in Waco at the turn of the twentieth century. The 1900 U.S. Census showed that in addition to his wife and children, Deane had his seventy-three-year-old mother and his nine-year-old nephew living with him. Deane continued his photographic business in Waco until around 1906, when he relocated to Beaumont.

At some point between the turn of the twentieth century and the next national head count in 1910, Deane's family unraveled. The 1910 census showed him as a fifty-year-old divorced man living in Dallas, where he still made his living as a photographer. He had a second-floor studio at Elm and Ackard Streets until the fall of 1910, when a newspaper ad offered his business for sale at "a sacrifice" because he was "sick in sanitarium."

Deane's ex-wife and children had moved west to El Paso in 1909 after a short time in Denison. The 1912 El Paso City Directory listed Maude Deane as widowed, a status she likely preferred over being shown as divorced. Based on Maude's claim of being a widow, Deane may have died in the winter of 1910 or sometime in 1911. However, a 1916 ad in the *Waco Morning News* for J.C. Deane "Home portraits by Photography" indicates that he was still alive. Another indication that "One-Eyed" Deane might not have died in 1910–11 is that in August 1917, a J.C. Deane and two other men received a charter for a Dallas-based corporation known as the Liberty Film Company. The exact date of Deane's death remains a mystery, as does the location of the peregrinating photographer's final resting place.

Nonetheless, the images the Deanes and Bergstrom took of the Crash at Crush live on, having been published multiple times over the years. The only known surviving prints are among the holdings of Baylor University's Texas collection in Waco.

Enoch J. Rector

The man Crush contracted with to record the Katy crash on moving film finally found success in his chosen field, but he didn't make any real money off it. Still, film historians consider Enoch Rector a key figure both in technological development and the business model that made the motion picture industry possible.

The year after the Crash at Crush, Rector took his motion picture gear to Carson City, Nevada, for the March 17, 1897 prizefight pitting Bob Fitzsimmons against Jim Corbett. The light being favorable and the fight going fourteen rounds, Rector used three cameras to take eleven thousand feet of 63mm film. Back in New York, he edited the film to produce a ninety-minute documentary. Using a projector called the Veriscope, he showed the film in New York and then contracted for it to be shown on the road, reportedly earning hundreds of thousands of dollars. Debuting on May 22, 1897, the movie is considered the world's first feature film. It made more than $600,000, but he was denied his share of the profits.

Abandoning the filmmaking field, he spent the rest of his life as an inventor. He came up with several good ideas—an amateur movie camera, an inexpensive record player and a device he called the Rector Gasifier, which would allow a gas-powered engine to operate on less expensive fuel oil. But none led to financial success for their inventor.

Rector lived to ninety-four, dying in New York on January 26, 1957. Although not all of his fight film has survived, the only known remaining segments were transferred to 35mm film in the 1980s and later digitized. In 2012, the film was added to the Library of Congress's National Film Registry as a "culturally, historically or aesthetically significant film."

THE VICTIMS

Emma Frances Overstreet

When newspapers reported her death as a result of the Crush crash, slip-shod journalistic work resulted in the fifteen-year-old girl being identified as "Mrs. J.L. Overstreet," a farmer's wife.

In truth, Emma Frances Overstreet was the young daughter of John Lee Overstreet, a then sixty-year-old farmer and Civil War veteran who had come from Mississippi with his wife and family to farm in McLennan County. Emma had been born in Newton, Mississippi, on July 27, 1881, before the Overstreets moved to Texas. She had two older brothers, three older sisters, a younger brother and two younger sisters, but nothing else is known of her short life. Newspaper reports also erroneously had her standing one thousand yards from the scene when

Crash at Crush victim Emma Overstreet's grave in McLennan County, Texas. *Author's collection.*

struck in the head just above her right ear by a flying metal rod, but it was a piece of timber and the distance was not nearly that far. She fell to the

John Overstreet and his wife, parents of fifteen-year-old victim Emma Overstreet. *Author's collection.*

ground unconscious and her family and bystanders thought she was dead, but she came to briefly before she did die. Her place of death is listed as Axtell, a small town roughly fourteen miles southeast of West.

The teenager was buried at the Olive Branch Cemetery at the small community of LeRoy. Her tombstone has fallen over and is broken in two places.

Ernest L. Darnall

A prominent Bremond resident and stockman who fought for the South during the Civil War, John Darnall apparently was a man of some means. He could have afforded to file suit against the Katy seeking damages for his son's death, but for whatever reason, he did not. What he did do was pay for an expensive eight-foot gray granite marker for his son Ernest's grave. The inscription on the east-facing side of the obelisk told a sad story, and while not naming the railroad, it amounted to an everlasting public shaming of the MKT:

Ernest L.
Only Son of John W. and Novvie J.
Darnall
Born
Nov. 1, 1872
Was Wounded While
Witnessing The Col-
Lision At Crush, Tex

And Died In Waco

Sept. 16, 1896

The northern side of the monument bears these words:

A Precious One From
Us Has Gone.
A Voice We Loved Is
Stilled.
A Place Is Vacated In
Our Home.
Which Never Can Be
Filled.

Tombstone of Ernest L. Darnall in the Bremond, Texas Cemetery amounts to a public shaming of the Katy. The twenty-three-year-old died of a massive head wound the day after the Crash at Crush. *Photo by Mike Cox.*

What Darnall's tombstone doesn't reveal is that someone else almost died instead of him. One Egbert McFadden, who had come to Texas from Tennessee for his health, had climbed a tree to get a better view. Just before the crash, he decided he could see better from the ground and climbed down. Darnall took the vantage point he had vacated.

The elder Darnall only had to live with his grief for a little less than six years. He died at fifty-seven on August 14, 1902, and was buried next to his son beneath a much simpler monument.

John H. Morrison

When a McLennan County justice of the peace checked the mangled John Morrison's pockets hoping to find something to confirm his identity, the magistrate discovered an accidental death policy from Fidelity Casualty Company of New York. Whether Morrison had owned the policy long enough for it to have taken effect is not known, but it was in the amount of $3,000. Also unanswerable today is whether he had taken out the policy as a precaution for his family before leaving to see the Crush crash or whether its presence on his body was only a coincidence.

What is known is that Morrison was born on June 28, 1862, possibly in Wise County. His uncle, Hiram Morrison, was a well-known real estate agent, financier and horse speculator in Dallas who had come to Texas from North Carolina.

The younger Morrison ran a livery stable in Ferris and farmed. "John possessed many noble traits of character, was kind and generous hearted and had many friends who were shocked at the news of his sad fate and heartily sympathize with his mourning relatives and grief stricken wife and child," the *Ferris Wheel* commented in an article published four days after his death. He was buried at Patrick-Pruitt Cemetery, about three miles from Ferris in Dallas County.

DeWitt Clinton Barnes

Later tellings of the Crush story often listed a man named DeWitt Clinton Barnes of Hewitt, Texas, as one of the spectators killed that day. Like so many other Central Texas residents, the thirty-four-year-old Waco resident had indeed witnessed the smashup, but he survived the experience unscathed. Even so, he would not be living to old age—and his death would be eerily similar to the actual Crush fatalities.

Two years after the crash, as Barnes and his wife, Eleanor, rode in their buggy past a carnival playing in Waco, someone touched off a charge of black powder packed down the hole of a blacksmith's anvil. Known as "firing an anvil," this was common in Fourth of July and New Year's celebrations. The resulting explosion sounded like the roar of a small cannon. Unfortunately for Barnes on this day, whoever blew the anvil had put too much powder in the hole and the heavy hunk of metal exploded like a cannon ball. At bullet-like velocity, a piece of the shrapnel penetrated Barnes's skull, and he slumped over unconscious in the buggy seat. His wife took the reins from the hands of her husband and rushed to the residence of the friends they had been en route to visit. A doctor was summoned, but Barnes soon died.

The Professional Train Wrecker

Joe Connolly

The man who took Alfred Streeter's idea and turned it into his life's vocation died at eighty-nine on February 27, 1948, in Des Moines, Iowa. Only his elderly sister survived him, and she died in 1950.

Joe Connolly's hometown newspaper took no notice of the fact that he had destroyed 146 locomotives in seventy-three staged train wrecks. The *Des Moines Register* only offered that Connolly "was in the theatrical business for more than 40 years, managing early-day theaters in Des Moines."

The Connolly farm, inherited by distant relatives, was leased by the family for nearly four decades until the man working the land bought it in 1987. The farm home where Connolly had lived still stands, although it has been remodeled.

"Head-On" Joe Connolly's last crash at the Iowa State Fair in 1932. *Iowa State Fair.*

Connolly and his wife, Margaret, lie beneath a simple tombstone in Des Moines's St. Ambrose Cemetery. No historical marker commemorates Connolly's unusual career, but the Iowa State Fair Museum in Des Moines has on display a steam locomotive bell found at his farm after his death.

The Last Witness

The last known witness to the Crash as Crush lived to be ninety-seven, dying on January 7, 1983. Her name was Ludmila (Milly) A. Smajstria Nemecek. Born on June 1, 1885, she was eleven when she saw the crash and escaped unscathed. "My parents, my two brothers and I went to the event in a wagon," she said in a 1979 interview. "Oh, there were so many people there—so much excitement....I've never forgotten what all that stuff up in the air looked like."

She is buried at Saint Mary's Catholic Cemetery in West, only a few miles from the site of the crash. With her death, the Crash at Crush faded from living memory.

Artifacts

Yesterday's souvenirs are today's archaeological artifacts. Waco historian Roger Conger, who wrote a paper on the Crash at Crush for the Waco Historical Society, used a metal detector to locate the site of the crash so that a state historical marker could be placed there in 1977. In searching the area, he dug up twenty-five to thirty pounds of what he called "shrapnel." Conger died at eighty-five in 1996, and what became of those artifacts is not known. Of the hundreds of pieces of wreckage carried off from Crush, only a few have been described or are known today.

In the 1950s, Milton C. Morgan, son-in-law of E.E. Dickenson, who inherited the western side of the crash site from his father, used to find chunks of train debris while plowing. He said they'd be six to eight inches deep and that every time he hit one, he'd have to climb off his tractor and pick it up.

For years, D.J. Price, who traveled from Palestine in East Texas to see the crash, kept a small brass oil cup that had been converted to an ink well.

Cartoon depiction of the Crash at Crush published in 1939. Forty years went by before the story of the Crash at Crush began to be retold. *Author's collection.*

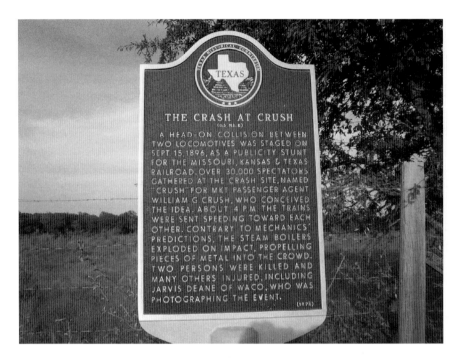

Crash at Crush state historical marker that now stands outside the old Katy depot in West, Texas. The 1977 marker originally stood near the crash site but was later moved to West. *Author's collection.*

Witness Clitus Jones of Dallas, who saw the crash as a child, said in 1956 that for years his family used a gilded piece of metal from one of the trains as a door stop. What became of those relics is not known.

One of the more enthusiastic collectors of Crush artifacts was Alfred E. Gerik (1924–2010), longtime chief of West's volunteer fire department. His uncle had witnessed the crash, and hearing stories about it inspired his interest in the event and its aftermath. As the 100th anniversary of the event approached in 1996, Gerik told the *Waco Tribune-Herald* that those present that day never forgot seeing a sky full of falling debris. People who did not attend never stopped regretting it, he said.

The History of West Museum at 112 East Oak in West, Texas, has an unidentified train part found by farmer Emil Hutyra. The family of John Foit, who leased land to the Katy for the event, still has a piece that supposedly was part of the cradle beneath one of the locomotive bells.

Left: West, Texas museum volunteer Pat Lassetter with a piece of one of the locomotives destroyed in the Crash at Crush. *Photo by Mike Cox.*

Below: Closeup of one of the few Crash at Crush artifacts. *Photo by Mike Cox.*

THE LAST CRASH

The national made-to-order train crash fad continued for only a short time after "Head-On" Connolly engineered his final wreck. The Minnesota State Fair at St. Paul featured crashes in 1933 and again in 1934, but only one more followed after that. The final known pay-to-see crash was a desperate effort on the part of a small failing railroad, the Rutland, Toluca & Northern, to raise cash. The planners chose a location near Magnolia, Illinois, arranged for two used locomotives from another line and ran them together on June 30, 1935. But too many people found places where they could see the crash for free. On top of that, the engines didn't reach the desired speed before impact, and the resulting crash was ho-hum compared with so many of the previous spectacles. Born during one economic depression, railroad crashing for fun and profit died during another, even more severe, depression.

GOODBYE, KATY

The MKT had the reputation of being a tolerably well-run railroad, but it always had a lot of competition and as a business venture never enjoyed a consistently smooth ride.

In September 1915, for the first time since shortly before Crush started with the railroad in 1893, the Katy went into receivership. Then, during World War I, it was under federal control, as were all other U.S. carriers. On April 1, 1923, the line was reorganized as the Missouri-Kansas-Texas Railroad and in the process lost some of its trackage. Still, the Katy operated under able leadership, with its freight and passenger trains running on 2,787 miles of track.

When the nation's economy derailed during the Great Depression, the MKT kept running without having to take the bankruptcy option. In fact, from 1929—the year the stock market crashed—through 1931, the Katy's annual net profit remained in the black. Beginning in 1931, however, the company operated at a deficit. What probably saved the line was a $3 million Reconstruction Finance Corporation loan in 1938. Some maintained that the Katy would have been smarter to go into receivership once again, cut costs as much as possible (i.e., layoffs, purchase little or no new rolling stock and defer maintenance) and eliminate all the debt it could. But the Katy opted for the federal loan and survived the Depression.

Left: Monument commemorating the Katy's history stands in the courtyard of the old MKT Depot in Denison. *Photo by Mike Cox.*

Below: Once a bustling train station, the former MKT Depot in Denison now houses the Red River Railroad Museum, dedicated to the Katy. *Photo by Mike Cox.*

Still running but with a bare-bones budget, the company stayed with the lighter, ninety-pounds-per-yard (or less) rails it had and avoided adding new equipment. Consequently, the line could not handle the heavier freight trains of the era, and its competitors benefited from that while the Katy lost out on the opportunity for the increased revenue born of better traffic volume.

By 1940, all that became someone else's worry as Crush finally retired. During World War II, the Katy did its part in the war effort and, in the process, made money. But the heavy traffic wore out its trackage. After the war, the company failed to invest in new infrastructure and maintenance. However, the company did begin converting to diesels. In 1948, the railroad ordered a streamlined diesel-electric engine and new coaches for its signature passenger train, the Texas Special, as well as its other passenger trains. By 1953, the Katy had phased out the last of its steam locomotives.

Despite the Katy's efforts to improve its passenger trains, airplanes were becoming increasingly streamlined in their own way, and as commercial air travel became more popular, passenger rail travel declined. In the early 1960s, the nation's railroads realized that they were in a hopeless situation and began an incremental shutdown of their people-hauling business.

In May 1965, John Barringer III took over as MKT's president and oversaw the final few months of the Katy's long history of passenger service. In the end, what finally killed the company's role as a provider of public transportation was the U.S. Post Office Department. As a cost-cutting measure, the government began using trucks rather than passenger trains in carrying mail. In Texas, Katy's mail contract amounted to 60 percent of its passenger service revenue. When the government money went away, the MKT's passenger service amounted to a dead letter, its trains carrying mostly die-hard older passengers or people afraid of flying.

Barringer told the Association Press that the Katy's passenger trains had been providing no "appreciable public service" and that their discontinuance would enable the line to spend money on upgrading its trackage and facilities. The average run from Dallas to Kansas City, he said, carried only ten passengers. The Interstate Commerce Commission granted the Katy's request to end its passenger service from Dallas to Kansas City effective June 30, 1965, and the Texas Railroad Commission approved the company's request to abandon its service between Dallas and San Antonio. That also ended passenger service in Waco, Temple and Austin. In all, seventy communities in Texas, Oklahoma, Kansas and Missouri were without passenger service for the first time since the Katy came to Texas in 1872.

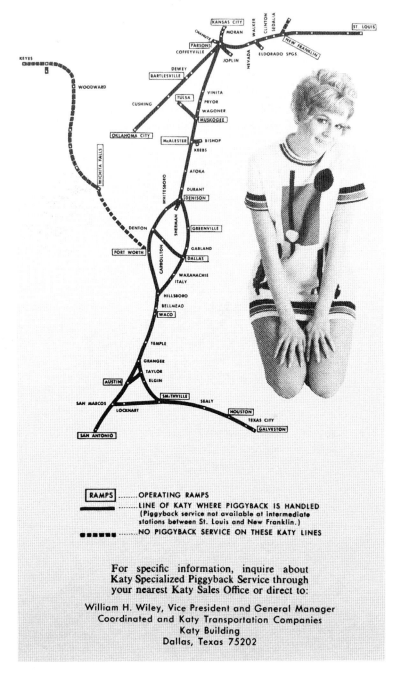

RAMPS .... OPERATING RAMPS

──── .... LINE OF KATY WHERE PIGGYBACK IS HANDLED
(Piggyback service not available at intermediate
stations between St. Louis and New Franklin.)

▬▬▬▬▬ .... NO PIGGYBACK SERVICE ON THESE KATY LINES

For specific information, inquire about
Katy Specialized Piggyback Service through
your nearest Katy Sales Office or direct to:

William H. Wiley, Vice President and General Manager
Coordinated and Katy Transportation Companies
Katy Building
Dallas, Texas 75202

Even after discontinuing its passenger service in 1965, the MKT kept the
Katy girl in its corporate advertising. In this 1970 image, Katy is a thoroughly
modern woman, the big hat and ankle-covering dress of the 1890s long gone.
Author's collection.

The old Katy Depot at West, Texas, the nearest permanent depot to the crash site at the short-lived town of Crush, Texas. The West depot has been restored, but trains roll on through without stopping. *Photo by Mike Cox.*

Although the AP report on the discontinuance of the MKT's passenger service did note that it marked the end of an era, the dispatch was only four paragraphs long. While some veteran Katy employees doubtless mourned the end of the line's once first-rate passenger trains, and old-time Texans may have waxed nostalgic about the change, for most people the disappearance of passenger trains that William G. Crush had worked so long and hard to promote was more like hearing that someone who had been suffering from a terminal disease had finally succumbed to his or her affliction. The end did not come as a shock.

One man who particularly mourned the demise of the Katy's passenger trains was Allen Duckworth. And being political editor of one of the Southwest's largest and best-regarded newspapers, he did so publicly in the June 28, 1965, edition of the *Dallas Morning News*.

"Katy has been host to the great in the professions, in the industries, in the affairs of state—men like Dwight D. Eisenhower, Harry Truman, Sam Rayburn," he wrote. In fact, not long after the December 7, 1941 attack on Pearl Harbor, then Colonel Eisenhower was on his way to Washington in a military plane. Grounded in Dallas by bad weather, he caught the Katy for St. Louis for a connecting train to the capital.

Duckworth recalled with mouthwatering fondness the meals prepared on Katy passenger trains. "No railroad in the nation had a dining car service which eclipsed the Katy when it was at its peak," he wrote. What he particularly relished were the "cornettes…dainty, tasty little cornbread muffins, cake-like, delicious." At night, passengers were given an apple to tide them over until breakfast miles down the line.

"Many a homesick Texan, longing to be with his family, became a little weepy-eyed when he approached the night train at the St. Louis station and saw the steaming rear-end with its herald, 'Texas Special,'" he wrote.

Not long after the last Katy passenger train pulled out of Dallas, the railroad shuttered Crush's Highland Park station, and it was soon razed. That left Frank Wakefield, who had begun his career with the Katy as a Pullman car attendant, without a job. He had been station master at Highland Park for forty years. "At a time," he told a reporter, "we were the best railroad in the world."

Since the line had been losing $3.75 million per year on the Dallas–San Antonio route, and probably about the same on its Dallas–Kansas City route, the end of passenger service did help the Katy's bottom line. The year before Barringer had taken over, gross revenue had been $56 million. In 1968, free from running passenger trains, gross revenue hit $68 million. Despite his successes, Barringer realized the Katy's best hope was to find a "husband" in the form of a merger.

When Barringer retired in 1970, new MKT president Reginald Whitman started shutting down the system's money-losing freight routes. That did bring a spike in revenue, but various rail mergers had left the Katy trapped in an iron net formed by larger companies—Santa Fe–Burlington Northern, Southern Pacific and Union Pacific. Finally, in 1988, Union Pacific bought the MKT and merged it into its system.

With the corporate absorption of the Katy, the Southwest lost more than a longtime railroad that had contributed so much to the region's development. It lost much of the company's history.

When Union Pacific took over the Katy, the scene at the railroad's offices was reminiscent of the sacking of Rome, minus the toppling of statues. Offices, desks and file cabinets, as one passerby later reported, were being "ruthlessly cleared out following the sale of the railroad to the Union Pacific." Papers and files were being tossed into plastic chutes leading to dumpsters, the railroad's records sliding down from the upper floors into

The Union Pacific Railroad now operates on these tracks in the vicinity of the 1896 collision at Crush. *Photo by Mike Cox.*

oblivion. Fortunately for posterity, a railroad buff collected some of the documents—including the original blueprints for the Katy's 1917-vintage depot in San Antonio—but most of the paperwork that told the Katy story ended up in landfills.

More than twenty years before the Katy came to the end of the line, the *Dallas Morning News*' political editor, who as a journalist had traveled many a mile on MKT passenger trains, put the Katy story into a perspective that holds up well: "The Katy has been a brave railroad, at times mismanaged, once used for financial greed-gain during its domination by Jay Gould. But it has made a contribution to the civilization of this part of the country—in Kansas, Missouri, Oklahoma and Texas."

And, he continued, there was one more thing for which the MKT should be remembered: "The Katy is probably the only railroad which had casualties in a planned wreck."

KNOWN STAGED LOCOMOTIVE CRASHES IN THE UNITED STATES

I f professional train crash promoter "Head-On" Joe Connolly kept a listing of all the locomotive crashes he staged, it is not known to have survived. This partial list is based on the two published booklets on Connolly's crashes (see bibliography) and contemporary newspaper articles. Seventy-one crashes or unconfirmed advertised crashes by Alfred Streeter, Connolly and others have been identified here. Since Connolly claimed to have staged seventy-three crashes himself, obviously some events are yet to be identified.

May 30, 1896	Columbus, OH	Buckeye Park, Alfred L. Streeter
July 4, 1896	Cicero, IL	A.L. Streeter
July 25, 1896	Chicago, IL	A.L. Streeter
August 1896	Corydon, IN	Local fair, promoter unknown
September 9, 1896	Des Moines, IA	Joe Connolly's first crash
September 15, 1896	Crush, TX	MKT RR; first staged crash west of the Mississippi
September 18, 1896	Sioux City, IA	Local fair, promoter unknown
September 27, 1896	Evanston, IA	A.L. Streeter

September 30, 1896	Denver, CO (Elyria)	William Jennings Bryan presidential campaign fundraiser
October 6, 1896	Kansas City, MO	Kansas City Karnival Krewe, Joe Connolly
April 7, 1897	Tampa, FL	D.D. Kinnebrew (advertised)
May 28, 1898	Buckeye Park, OH	A.L. Streeter
July 4, 1900	Indianapolis, IN	Amalgamated Order of Trainmen
July 4, 1900	Buffalo, NY	Rochester Driving Park, E.W. Oviatt, manager
1900	Boston, MA	Joe Connolly
September 10, 1902	Milwaukee, WI	Wisconsin State Fair, Joe Connolly
September 23, 1902	Louisville, KY	Kentucky State Fair, Joe Connolly
August 1, 1903	Fort Wayne, IN	Railroad Carnival (advertised), promoter unknown
September 1903	Louisville, KY	Kentucky State Fair, Joe Connolly
1903	Boston, MA	Joe Connolly
July 4, 1904	Point of Pines, ME	William O'Neill and Boston & Maine RR
November 1904	San Antonio, TX	International Fair, Joe Connolly
November 26, 1905	San Antonio, TX	International Fair, Joe Connolly
May 3, 1906	Topeka, KS	State Fair (advertised), Joe Connolly?
July 4, 1906	Brooklyn, NY	Brighton Beach Racetrack, Joe Connolly
September 10, 1906	Los Angeles, CA	James Morley, Walter Hempel

May 29, 1907	Wilkes-Barre, PA	Manhattan Beach (advertised), promoter unknown
July 1907	Brooklyn, NY	Brighton Beach Racetrack, Joe Connolly
October 13, 1907	Fort Worth, TX	Second Annual Fort Worth Fair, Joe Connolly
1907	Oklahoma City, OK	Joe Connolly
1907	St. Joseph, MO	Joe Connolly
1907	Milwaukee, WI	Joe Connolly
November 17, 1907	San Antonio, TX	International Fair, Joe Connolly
November 1908	San Antonio, TX	International Fair, Joe Connolly
February 3, 1909	Jacksonville, FL	Exposition Fair, Joe Connolly
July 4, 1911	Indianapolis, IN	State Fair, Joe Connolly
1911	Brooklyn, NY	Brighton Beach Racetrack, Joe Connolly
September 16, 1911	Louisville, KY	State Fair, Joe Connolly
August 1912	Milwaukee, WI	State Fair, Joe Connolly
September 1912	Louisville, KY	State Fair, Joe Connolly
September 16, 1913	Chattanooga, TN	Grand Army of the Republic Reunion, Joe Connolly
September 17, 1913	Sacramento, CA	State Fair, H.R. Wright, Sacramento Citizens Committee
September 8, 1914	Phillipsburg, PA	Crash filmed by Sigmund Lubin, owner of Lubin Film Company, Philadelphia and used in two silent movies
September 16, 1914	Sacramento, CA	State Fair, H.R. Wright, Sacramento Citizens Committee

September 6, 1915	Omaha, NE	Omaha Auto Speedway, Joe Connolly
September 6, 1915	Joplin, MO	Schifferdecker Park, promoter unknown
July 4, 1916	Tacoma, WA	Tacoma Speedway (advertised), promoter unknown
September 4, 1916	Sacramento, CA	State Fair, promoter unknown
September 5, 1917	Sacramento, CA	State Fair, promoter unknown
October 1, 1919	Fresno, CA	Promoter unknown
September 4, 1920	St. Paul, MN	State Fair, Joe Connolly
June 11, 1921	Portland, OR	Rose City Speedway (advertised), promoter unknown
September 3, 1921	St. Paul, MN	State Fair, Joe Connolly
August 26, 1922	Des Moines, IA	State Fair, Joe Connolly
August 29, 1925	Aurora, IL	Central States Fair, Joe Connolly
February 22, 1931	Miami, FL	Miami Junior Chamber of Commerce Summer Tourism Committee
August 27, 1932	Des Moines, IA	Iowa State Fair, Joe Connolly's last crash
September 8, 1933	St. Paul, MN	State Fair, State Fair Association
September 7, 1934	St. Paul, MN	State Fair, State Fair Association
June 30, 1935	Magnolia, IL	Rutland, Toluca & Northern RR
July 17, 1951	Durango, CO	Two obsolete Denver & Rio Grande locomotives crashed together during filming of *Denver & Rio Grande*, released in 1952

No Date/Pre-1932

Atlanta, GA	Joe Connolly
Cincinnati, OH	Joe Connolly
Detroit, MI	Joe Connolly
Grand Rapids, MI	Joe Connolly
Kankakee, IL	Joe Connolly
Lincoln, NE	Joe Connolly
Macon, GA	Joe Connolly
Pittsburgh, PA	Joe Connolly
Salt Lake City, UT	Joe Connolly
Toledo, OH	Joe Connolly

SOURCE NOTES

PROLOGUE

Author's interview with Patricia Cloud, West, Texas, September 28, 2017. Mrs. Cloud is Joseph Foit's granddaughter.

Joseph Foit was born on August 5, 1887, in West, Texas, and died on November 20, 1968, in Hillsboro, Texas. Like his father, he had spent most of his life as a farmer. His father, John Foit (1851–1929), had come to Texas from the area of eastern Europe that would later become Czechoslovakia. One of Foit's descendants still owns a portion of the original homestead.

KATY COMES TO TEXAS

Houston Chronicle, "Engineer at Throttle 60 Years Ago to Be in Katy Special Cab Today," December 25, 1932.

Fort Worth Star-Telegram, "Denison to Celebrate Christmas First Train Advent 60 Years Ago," December 25, 1932.

MKT Employees Magazine, "Sixty Years Ago This Month Katy Ran First Train into Texas" (December 1932): 4; "Whistle of Katy's First Train Heralded Development of Texas" (December 1932): 4–5.

Hunt, *Frontier Denison, Texas*, 11–20.

Nashville Union and American, "Missouri, Kansas and Texas Railway," November 16, 1872.

Cairo Bulletin, "Greeting to the Outside World," December 25, 1872.

Waterville (KS) Telegraph, March 28, 1873.

Chicago Tribune, June 18, 1873.

Scribner's Monthly 6, no. 3, "Great South," 257–88.
Missouri-Kansas-Texas Railroad, *Opening of the Great Southwest.*
Fort Worth Gazette, "The Katy Reduction," February 7, 1894.
Masterson, *Katy Railroad and the Last Frontier.*
Collias, *Katy Power*, 7–30.
Hunt and Bryant, *Denison*, 29–38.
Drury, *Guide to North American Steam Locomotives*, 215–17.
Bracken, *Historic McLennan County*, 72–74.
Texas Transportation Museum, "History (Missouri-Kansas-Texas—MKT),"
    www.txtransportationmuseum.org/history-rr-missouri-kansas-texas.php.
Medallion, "Tex-Czechs," 8–11.
Kathryn Devers Doherty and Shirley Kubala, "West, TX," Handbook of Texas
    Online, http://www.tshaonline.org/handbook/online/articles/hgw06.
City of West, Texas, "Our History," http://www.cityofwest.com/our-history
Find A Grave, "Thomas Marion West (1834–1912)," www.findagrave.com/
    memorial/19433229/thomas-marion-west.

THE NOT-SO-GAY NINETIES

Brands, *Reckless Decade.*
Hirsch and Goler, *City Comes of Age.*
Kasson, *Buffalo Bill's Wild West*, 93–105.
Larson, *Devil in the White City.*
Saylor Academy, "Panic of 1893," https://resources.saylor.org/wwwresources/
    archived/site/wp-content/uploads/2011/08/HIST312-10.1.2-Panic-
    of-1893.pdf.
Foundation for Economic Education, "The Silver Panic," https://fee.org/
    articles/the-silver-panic.
Stephens, *Historical Atlas of Texas*, 241.
Waco Morning News, "The Nation's Unemployed," January 1, 1894.
Galveston Daily News, "Feed the Hungry," January 2, 1894.
Waco Morning News, "To Give the Destitute Work," January 19, 1894.
United States History. "The Silver Question." https://www.u-s-history.
    com/pages/h763.html.

WORKIN' ON THE RAILROAD

Brann, "Locomotive Engineer," *Brann the Iconoclast*, 119–23.
Reinhardt, *Workin' on the Railroad*, 123.
American Railroads, 149, 151–52.
Philpott, *Cinder in Your Eye*, 3.

Phillips, *Yonder Comes the Train*, 372, 377.

Ogburn, *Railroads*, 130.

Ben Sargent e-mail to author, August 28, 2018.

RAILROAD WRECK MADE TO ORDER

Encyclopedia of Chicago, "Railroad Supply Industry," www.encylopedia. chicagohistory.org/pages2387.

Mark J. Price, "Local History: Trains Collided for Fun and Profit in Late 19th Century," *Akron (OH) Beacon Journal*, July 13, 2014.

Akron (OH) Beacon Journal, "A Terrible Collision," July 13, 1895.

Canton (OH) Repository, "A Few Facts Regarding the Great Railway Collision," July 18, 1895.

Canton (OH) Repository, "A Huge Farce," July 21, 1895.

Marion (OH) Star, "The Colliding Engines," May 6, 1896.

Chicago Tribune, "Wreck Two Trains for Amusement," May 31, 1896.

Chicago Tribune, "Railroad Collision for Pastime," June 2, 1896.

New York World, "Railroad Wreck Made to Order, Unique and Costly Entertainment Provided for the Opening of a Park in Ohio, Collision of Engines Going 50 Miles an Hour," June 7, 1896.

Joyce Harvey, "Buckeye Park and a Demolition Derby on Steroids," *Lancaster (OH) Eagle-Gazette*, September 7, 2014; "Buckeye Park's Last 100 Years," *Lancaster (OH) Eagle-Gazette*, October 12, 2014.

Roger Pickenpaugh, "Opportunity of a Lifetime," *Timeline Magazine* 15, no. 2 (1998).

Chicago Inter Ocean, "Crowds Enjoy a Collision," July 5, 1896.

Chicago Tribune, "Railroad Collision to be Repeated," July 13, 1896.

Chicago Tribune, "Engines for the Collision Here," July 16, 1896.

Chicago Tribune, "Political Angle in the Collision," July 25, 1896

Chicago Inter Ocean, July 26, 1896.

Alton (IL) Telegraph, "A Unique Exhibition," July 30, 1896.

J.M. Farnham to B.C. Murray, *Denison Sunday Gazetteer*, September 6, 1896.

A MAN WITH A VERY APROPOS NAME

U.S. Census Records, 1870, Louisville, Jackson County, Kentucky; 1880, Louisville, Jackson County, Kentucky; 1900, Dallas, Dallas County, Texas; 1910, Dallas, Dallas County; 1920, Highland Park, Dallas County, Texas; 1930, Highland Park, Dallas County, Texas.

Texas Death Certificate, Dallas County, Texas.

Dallas Morning News, October 17, 1897.

Railway Agent and Station Agent, "Courteous and Gentlemanly G.P.A," 202.

Denison Sunday Gazetteer, "Crush Crowned," October 1, 1893.

St. Louis Post-Dispatch, "To Fight Houston," October 5, 1893.

Raymond George Jr., "Origin of the Katy Flyer: The Katy's First Named Train," *Katy Flyer* (December 2014): 8–9.

Dallas Morning News, "Is Over at Last: Head-End Collision Is a Thing of the Past," September 16, 1896.

Who's Who in Railroading in North America. New York: Simmons-Boardman Publishing Corporation, 1930, 116.

MKT Employee Magazine, "W.G. Crush Did Much in 40 Years," 8–9.

The Sincerest Form of Flattery

Dallas Morning News, August 5, 1896.

Dallas Times-Herald, "A Collision. Two Trains on the Katy Dash Head Ends Together. Billy Crush Comes Home. Tells of the Head-Ender that Is Being Gotten Up," August 12, 1896.

Denison Sunday Gazetteer, "Don't Miss This," August 23, 1896.

Fort Scott (KS) Daily Monitor, "The Head End Collision," September 2, 1896.

Governor Charles Culberson's correspondence files at the Texas State Library and Archives in Austin, Boxes 301-156 and 301-157, June 1, 1896, through December 31, 1896, contain no letter of invitation to the governor from Crush or anyone else with the MKT. In fact, there is no correspondence related to the Crash at Crush. Donaly Brice to author, e-mail, June 5, 2018.

Building Steam

Dallas Times-Herald, September 1, 1896.

Dallas Times-Herald, "Off for Crush," September 1, 1896.

Sedalia (MO) Democrat, "September 15 Is the Date," September 3, 1896.

Parsons (KS) Daily Eclipse, September 14, 1896.

Galveston News, "They Are All Ready," September 15, 1896.

Dallas Morning News, "Is Over at Last."

Barnes, "Train Wreck," 14–17.

Sedalia (MO) Democrat, "Katy's Collision," September 11, 1896.

Dallas Morning News, "The Crash at Crush," September 15, 1896.

San Antonio Light, "The Katy Wreck," September 15, 1896.

Due to a paucity of MKT records, the first name of the Katy engineer who supposedly warned that a boiler explosion could follow Crush's planned head-on collision is not known. Surviving corporate records do show that a Leslie Arthur Hanrahan (born in 1907) worked as a laborer for the line (his start date was not shown) and left employment in July 1951. His father was listed as John Willis Hanrahan. Since it was not unusual for a son to follow in his father's footsteps in the railroad world, Red River Railroad Museum director Roy Jackson believes it possible that John Willis Hanrahan could have been the engineer whose judgment had been correct. Roy Jackson e-mail to author, July 17, 2018.

"The Most Novel Experiment Ever Given in Texas"

Houston Chronicle, "Katy Locomotive Crash in '96 Seen by Thousands," April 19, 1936.

Dallas Morning News, "Is Over at Last."

Galveston News, "Crush Collision," September 16, 1896.

Houston Post, "The Collision at Crush," September 16, 1896.

Marshall (TX) Evening Messenger, "The Crash at Crush," September 16, 1896.

Bryan (TX) Eagle, "The Crash at Crush," September 1, 1896.

Dallas Times-Herald, "One Person Killed," September 16, 1896.

Parsons (KS) Daily Eclipse, "The Collision at Crush," September 17, 1896.

Austin Statesman, "The Great Katy Collision," September 17, 1896.

Daily Ardmoreite (OK), "A Grand Sight," September 17, 1896.

Galveston News, September 17, 1896.

Temple Times, September 18, 1896.

Waco Weekly Tribune, September 19, 1896.

Waco News-Tribune, "Thousands Watched When Katy Staged Famed Train Wreck 60 Years Ago," September 6, 1956.

Rogers, "Pre-Arranged Head End Collision."

C.B. Smith to author, August 16, 1977.

Dallas Morning News, October 1, 1896.

W.M. Barrow, "Great Train Wreck," *Waco Tribune-Herald*, October 30, 1949.

MKT Employees Magazine, "Retired Katy Engineer Tells of Wreck at Crush" (September 1950): 11, 13.

Thomas Turner, "Train Wreck that Boomeranged," *Dallas Morning News*, August 8, 1954.

Dallas Morning News, "Crash at Crush Was Big Event," June 22, 1959.

George Carmac and Bonnie Carmac, "The Great Train Wreck at Crush," *San Antonio Express*, November 3, 1979.

"A SCENE THAT WILL HAUNT A MAN"

Barnes, "Train Wreck," 14–17.

Frank X. Tolbert, "Tolbert's Texas: Fireman Speaks on 'Crush's Crash,'" *Dallas Morning News*, February 3, 1963.

Frank X. Tolbert, "Eye Witnesses Tell of Crush's Crash," *Dallas Morning News*, May 6, 1956.

Houston Chronicle, "Katy Locomotive Crash in '96."

Dallas Morning News, "Mrs. Deane on the Crush Collision," October 1, 1896.

Connally, *Crash at Crush*.

Galveston News, September 16, 1896.

Dallas Morning News, "Crush Collision: The Force of the Blow and the Damage Done," September 17, 1896.

Waco Weekly Tribune, September 19, 1896.

Denison Sunday Gazetteer, "The Big Wreck," September 20, 1896.

Rogers, "Pre-Arranged Head End Collision," 125–29.

At the time of the Crash at Crush, Waco, Texas, had three vigorously competing newspapers that would have given the spectacle extensive coverage. But with the exception of the *Waco Weekly Tribune* for September 19, published four days after the crash, no Waco newspapers from 1896 have been located.

PICKING UP THE PIECES

Tolbert, "Eye Witnesses Tell of Crush's Crash."

Dallas Morning News, "Is Over at Last."

Dallas Morning News, "Crush Collision."

Dallas Morning News, "Statement from Crush," September 17, 1896.

Dallas Morning News, "Two Injured from Waxahachie," September 17, 1896.

Sedalia (MO) Democrat, September 18, 1896.

Dallas Morning News, "Round About Town," September 18, 1896.

Dallas Morning News, "Watch Was Found," September 18, 1896.

Dallas Times-Herald, "Dynamite," September 18, 1896.

Dallas Morning News, "Death-Dealing Chain," September 19, 1896.

Houston Post, September 19, 1896.

Daily Ardmoreite (Indian Territory), September 17, 1896.

J.E. Fee, "The South's Only Planned Train Wreck," *Dallas Morning News*, November 22, 1931.

Larry Knapek, "100th Anniversary of 'Crash at Crush', One of the Greatest Publicity Stunts of U.S. History," *West News*, September 12, 1996.

Owned by Louis H. Walter and Valentine Hafner, the Hillsboro jewelry and piano company served as the official watch inspector for both the MKT and the Trinity and Brazos Valley Railroad. All railroads required conductors and engineers to carry a watch that met agreed-on railroad standards. That watch had to be inspected for accuracy every two weeks, and a railroad worker had to produce the certificate if requested. The emphasis on accurate timepieces was to reduce the chance of head-on collisions.

A contemporary newspaper report noted that Justice of the Peace J.B. Earle said he would thoroughly investigate the deaths that followed the crash. Unfortunately, McLennan County has no justice court records for any of its precincts prior to 1937.

The Photographers

U.S. Census Records, 1860, Bethany, Brooks County, Virginia (now West Virginia); 1880, Kansas City, Jackson County, Missouri; 1900, Waco, McLennan County, Texas; 1910, Dallas, Dallas County, Texas.

Waco Evening News, September 21, 1881.

McLennan County Marriage Records, 1887.

Waco City Directory, 1896.

Gonzalez, "Jervis C. Deane."

Memorial and Biographical History of McLennan, Falls, Bell and Coryell Counties, 553–54.

Shreveport (LA) Times, "Remarkable Recovery," October 2, 1896.

Houston Post, "Deane's Wonderful Recovery," October 3, 1896.

Terri Jo Ryan, "Brazos Past: Waco's Wild World of 19th Century Photography," *Waco Tribune*, December 15, 2012.

Galveston News, "The Kinetoscope Play," February 28. 1896.

Hawley, *Fight that Started the Movies*, 97–103, 314–15.

The two uninjured Deane brothers apparently went to their brothers' studio in Waco and made prints either on the night of the crash or the following day. The September 17, 1896 edition of the *Dallas Morning News* published a series of three line engravings depicting the crash, the captions of each noting "From an instantaneous photograph." The *News* had a bureau in Waco, and it is possible that the correspondent sent a set of the images to Dallas by train for a newspaper staff artist to make engravings from them.

It is possible the Deanes or Bergstrom took more than five photographs. One of the illustrations accompanying the first magazine article on the crash, published in *Cosmopolitan* in December 1896, appears to be a pre-crash shot of the crowd before the trains arrived for their final "salute." In the corner of the image can be seen a camera on a tripod. If the image is based on a Deane photo, an original print of that image may not have survived. An article on the Crash at Crush in the October 30, 1949 edition of the *Waco News-Tribune* said that Louis Crow, who in the 1940s still operated a laundry in Waco with his brother, had also been on the photography platform when the locomotives collided. He had been using either a Kodak box camera, first produced in 1889, or a smaller Pocket Kodak, which hit the market in 1895. Whatever camera he had with him at the crash, the photographs he took are not believed to have survived.

LITIGATION AHEAD

Dallas Times-Herald, September 18, 1896.
Sedalia (MO) Democrat, "A Dangerous Thing," September 18, 1896.
Waco Weekly Tribune, September 19, 1896.
Artesia (Waco, TX) 6, no. 38, "Carnival of Death: How Railroad Royalty Amuses Itself" (September 20, 1896).
McLennan County, Texas Nineteenth Judicial District court records, cause no. 7361; cause no. 7436.
Art Chapman, "Crash at Crush," *Fort Worth Star-Telegram*, September 6, 1996.
Daily Ardmoreite (OK), September 16, 1896.
Dallas Morning News, "First Crush Suit Filed," September 20, 1896.
Shiner (TX) Gazette, September 24, 1896.
Dallas Morning News, "Crush Collision Damage Suit," October 4, 1896.
Sedalia (MO) Democrat, "A Suit for $16,800," October 19, 1896.
Galveston News, "The Katy's Answer," October 22, 1896.
Galveston News, "Crush Collision Judgment," November 14, 1896.
Austin Statesman, "Outgrowth of Crush Crash," November 14, 1896.

THE KING OF RAGTIME

Eric Ames, "Scott Joplin's 'Great Crush Collision March' and the Memorialization of a Marketing Spectacle," BU Libraries Digital Collections Blog, April 19, 2012, http:/blogs.baylor.edu/digitalcollections.
Berlin, *King of Ragtime*, 27–29.
Blesh and Janis, *They All Played Ragtime*, 43–44.
Kent Biffle, "Crush Crash Had Quite an Impact," *Dallas Morning News*, September 15, 1985.
Saint Paul (MN) Globe, "They Sing Well," November 2, 1893.

Boston Herald, "Herald Folk Serenaded," September 24, 1894.

Sedalia (MO) Democrat, "The Ragtime King," March 8, 1901.

Patricia Benoit to author, e-mails, March 11, 2018, August 23, 2018.

Ragtime Piano Recordings, Sheet Music Art, Nostalgia and Ragtime Research Resources Center, http://www.perfessorbill.com/pbmusic_joplin1.shtml

Given his surname, it's difficult to find much information on what became of Robert Smith. By February 1903, he had left Temple for Austin, where he was managing a piano store. He returned to Temple at some point but left again in October 1907 to manage the Barnes Music Company in Palestine. "Mr. Smith is an experienced man in the business, and is a pleasant gentleman to meet," the *Palestine Daily Herald* commented on October 18, 1907. Smith was shown in newspaper advertisements to be manager of the W.A. Leyhe Piano Company in Marshal, Texas, in 1910. After that, his whereabouts and how long he lived have not been determined.

John (Jack) R. Fuller was born on January 15, 1876, in Marlin, Falls County, Texas. When he brought out Joplin's Crush march, he was living at 104 North Eighth Street in Temple, just a short walk from the new MKT Depot and the club district, where Joplin may have been playing while he was in town. Fuller later moved from Temple to the small community of Mart, near Waco. There he and his cousin Thomas Whaley Patrick ran a music store. At some point, he drifted north from Texas, dying of complications from syphilis on November 26, 1915, in the State Mental Hospital in Deer Park, Montana. His remains were returned to his native state, where he was buried at Temple's Hillcrest Cemetery.

THE SHOW GOES ON…AND ON

Connolly, "I Wrecked 146 Locomotives."

Reisdorff, *Man Who Wrecked 146 Locomotives*.

Schmidt, *Train Wrecks for Fun and Profit*.

El Paso (TX) Herald, "Locomotive Collision as Fair Attraction," November 4, 1905.

For a man who generated so many newspaper stories during his train-smashing career, Joe "Head-On" Connolly received very little coverage himself. Although he surely must have been photographed, no images of him are known except for a poor-quality newspaper drawing that appeared in 1915.

End of the Line

Alfred L. Streeter

Arkansas Democrat, "Millionaire in a Bad Way," December 16, 1906.
Chicago Inter Ocean, "Runaway Girl Is Caught," October 14, 1906; "Declare
  Streeter in Canada," December 13, 1906; "Conspiracy Hinted in Miss
  Burkle Case," December 13, 1906; "Burkle Girl Tries to End Life; Caught
  at Marinette, Wis.," December 14, 1906; "Mrs. A.L. Streeter Urges Her
  Husband to Return," January 4, 1907; "In Exile for 3 Years; Streeter May
  Return," December 16, 1908.
Chicago Tribune, February 9, 1900; "Warrant for Man in Brooks Case,"
  August 31, 1906; "Girl from Rensu Tells Jury All," September 11, 1906;
  "Suicide of Business Man," December 2, 1906; "Official Probe for Burkle
  Case," December 16, 1906; "Decree Recalls Raid on Hotel to Rescue
  Girl," March 5, 1916.
Oshkosh (WI) Northwestern, "Streeter a Bigamist," December 15, 1906.
Muncie (IN) Evening Press, "Streeter's Millions Serve as Shield?" October 26,
  1907.
Pittsburgh Post-Gazette, "An Attempt to Prove Streeter a Bigamist," December
  15, 1906.

Alfred L. Streeter obtained railroad brake-related patents in 1897, 1899,
1900, 1903, 1904 (two), 1905, 1906, 1911, 1914, 1915 and 1916. U.S. Patent
Office, Washington, D.C.

W.G. Crush

Decatur (IL) Daily Review, "The Flying Katy," July 28, 1897.
Dallas Morning News, "W.G. Crush to Be Umpire," August 28, 1897.
Houston Post, "Passenger Agent Crush," October 16, 1897.
Houston Post, "William G. Crush," January 30, 1898.
Dallas Morning News, "Prominent Railroad Officials—W.G. Crush,"
  December 27, 1903.
St. Louis Post-Dispatch, "M-K-T Personnel Changes," October 1, 1930.
Texas Death Certificate, Dallas County, Texas.
Find A Grave, "William G. Crush," memorial no. 40023409.
Dallas Morning News, "W.G. Crush, Veteran Rail Man, Passes," April 13,
  1943.
Turner, *That's All for Today*, 247–49.
U.S. Census Records.

Charles Cain

Denison, Texas City Directory, U.S. City Directories.
Texas Select County Marriages.
1916 San Antonio City Directory, U.S. City Directories.
San Antonio Express, "Engineer Dies," March 8, 1925.
Texas Death Certificate.
Melissa Griswold e-mail to author, January 28, 2018.
U.S. 1910 Census, Bastrop County, Texas.

Charles Stanton

Waco News-Tribune, "Wacoan Who Aided in Famous Train Crash Stunt Dies," January 7, 1948.
Melissa Griswold e-mail to author, February 11, 2018.
Minnesota Marriage Index, 1849–1950.
Waco, Texas City Directory, 1917, U.S. City Directories.
U.S. Census Records, 1910, Bastrop County, Texas; 1920, Dallas, Dallas County, Texas; 1930, Waco, McLennan County, Texas.
Minnesota Death Index.

Frank Barnes

Waco Tribune-Herald, "Last Crewman Tells of 'Crash at Crush,'" December 4, 1955.
U.S. Census Records, 1870, Randolph County, Indiana; 1880; 1900, Bastrop County, Texas.
Texas Death Certificates.
Melissa Griswold e-mail to author, February 4, 2018.

S.M. Dickerson

Waco News Tribune, "S.M. Dickerson Funeral Rites Scheduled Today," January 13, 1955.
Waco News Tribune, "Mrs. Dickerson Celebrates 93rd Birthday," March 13, 1963.
Melissa Griswold e-mail to author, August 4, 2018.
U.S. Census Records, 1900, Hill County, Texas; 1910, Hill County, Texas; 1920, McLennan County, Texas.
U.S. Social Security Applications and Claims Index, 1937–2007.

Lowery Parsons

Melissa Griswold e-mail to author, December 17, 2017.
Edith Saunders, "'Turkey' Parsons Still Active at 101," *Austin American,* June 27, 1963.
Sherman, Denison City Directory, 1905, U.S. City Directories.
U.S. Census Records, 1880, Central Pickens, South Carolina; 1910, Hillsboro, Texas; 1920, Smithville, Bastrop County, Texas.
U.S. Social Security Applications and Claims Index, 1937–2007.

Frank Van Gilder

Houston Post, "He Is a Shriner," January 2, 1900.
Topeka Daily Capital, "Union Pacific Conductor Killed," December 4, 1902.
Melissa Griswold e-mail to author, February 4, 2018.
U.S. Census Records.

Thomas H. Webb

Houston Post, May 5, 1909; September 13, 1910; August 25, 1919.
U.S. Census Records, 1900, Hill County, Texas; 1910, Smithville, Bastrop County, Texas.
Melissa Griswold e-mail to author, January 6, 2018.

Jervis Deane

Memorial and Biographical History of McLennan, Falls, Bell and Coryell Counties, 553–54.

Enoch J. Rector

New York Times, "Enoch Rector, 94, Inventor, Dead. Aide of Edison on Sound Reproduction, Early Films, Designed Camera Shutter," January 27, 1957.

Emma Frances Overstreet

Find A Grave, "Emma Frances Overstreet," memorial no. 54511241.
Houston Post, September 20, 1896.

U.S. Census, 1880, Newton County, Mississippi; 1890, McLennan County, Texas.

Melissa Griswold e-mail to author, November 5, 2017.

Ernest L. Darnall

Find A Grave, "Ernest L. Darnall," memorial no. 66813345.

Austin Statesman, "Earnest Darnell [*sic*] Dead," September 17, 1896.

Melissa Griswold e-mail to author, November 19, 2017.

John H. Morrison

Find A Grave, "John H. Morrison," memorial no. 142403975.

Dallas Morning News, September 17, 1896.

Ferris (TX) Wheel, September 19, 1896.

U.S. Census, 1880, Ellis County, Texas.

DeWitt Barnes

Waco Tribune, May 13, 1898.

Melissa Griswold e-mail to author, December 17, 2017.

"Head-On" Joe Connolly

Reisdorff, *Man Who Wrecked 146 Locomotives*.

The Last Witness

Find A Grave, "Ludmila A. Smajstria Nemecek," memorial no. 44518658.

Artifacts

Waco Tribune-Herald, "Crash Sites Gets Marker," August 31, 1977

Dallas Morning News, "West Marker to be Dedicated," August 7, 1977.

Marla Pierson, "Duel of the Iron Monsters," *Waco Tribune-Herald*, September 15, 1996.

Tolbert, "Eye Witnesses Tell of Crush's Crash."

The Last Crash

Reisdorff, *Man Who Wrecked 146 Locomotives*.

Goodbye, Katy

Drury, *Guide to North American Steam Locomotives*, 215.
Allen Duckworth, "Katy to Close Passenger Era," *Dallas Morning News*, June 28, 1965.
Greenville Herald Banner, June 30, 1965.

BIBLIOGRAPHY

Unpublished Manuscripts

Gonzalez, Francisco J. "Jervis C. Deane: The Courage of Life." Typescript, n.d., Baylor University Texas Collection, Waco, Texas.

Pledger, Hal Warren. "Dewitt Barnes' Death." Typescript, April 5, 2006. Baylor University Texas Collection, Waco, Texas.

Government Documents

McLennan County, Texas Nineteenth Judicial District Docket Book, 1896. Cause No. 7436, *Roy Kendrick by Next Friend John D. Kendrick v. Missouri, Kansas & Texas Ry Co of Texas*, plaintiffs original petition, filed November 11, 1896. McLennan County Archives, Waco, Texas.

———. Cause No. 7361, *John L. Overstreet joined by his wife R.L. Overstreet v. Missouri, Kansas & Texas Ry Co of Texas*, plaintiffs original petition, filed October 15, 1896. McLennan County Archives, Waco, Texas.

McLennan County, Texas. Justice of the Peace Precinct 3 Docket Book, 1896. McLennan County Archives, Waco, Texas.

Minnesota Death Index. https://www.ancestry.com.

Minnesota Marriage Index, 1849–1950. https://www.ancestry.com.

Sixth Annual Report of the Railroad Commission of the State of Texas. Vol. 6, 1896–97. Austin, TX: Railroad Commission, 1898.

Texas Death Records. https://www.ancestry.com.
Texas Marriage Records. https://www.ancestry.com.
U.S. Census Records. https://www.ancestry.com.
U.S. Passport Records. https://www.ancestry.com.
U.S. Patent Records. https://www.uspto.gov.
U.S. Social Security Applications and Claims Index, 1937–2007.

CORPORATE DOCUMENTS

Missouri-Kansas-Texas Railroad Company Annual Report, 1896.
Missouri-Kansas-Texas Railroad Company Annual Report, 1948, 20–21.

THESIS

Ward, George B. "The Crash at Crush: Texas' Great Pre-Arranged Train Wreck." Master's thesis, University of Texas–Austin, May 1975.

BOOKS

Adams, Ramon F. *The Language of the Railroader*. Norman: University of Oklahoma Press, 1977.

The American Railway: Its Construction, Development, Management, and Appliances. New York: Charles Scribner's Sons, 1889.

Berlin, Edward A. *King of Ragtime: Scott Joplin and His Era*. New York: Oxford University Press, 1994.

Blesh, Rudi, and Harriet Janis. *They All Played Ragtime*. New York: Oak Publications, 1971, 1950.

Bracken, Sharon, ed. *Historic McLennan County: An Illustrated History*. San Antonio, TX: Historical Publishing Network, 2010.

Brands, H.W. *The Reckless Decade: America in the 1890s*. New York: St. Martin's Press, 1995.

Brann, W.C. "The Locomotive Engineer." In *Brann the Iconoclast: A Collection of the Writings of W.C. Brann in Two Volumes*. Waco, TX: Herz Brothers, 1898.

Collias, Joe G. *Katy Power: Locomotives and Trains of the Missouri-Kansas-Texas Railroad 1912–1985*. Crestwood, MO: MM Books, 1986.

Custer, Edgar A. *No Royal Road*. New York: H.C. Kinsey and Company Inc., 1937.

Drury, George H., comp. *Guide to North American Steam Locomotives*. Waukesha, WI: Kalmbach Books, 2015.

Fuhrman, Candice Jacobson. *Publicity Stunt! Great Staged Events that Made the News*. San Francisco, CA: Chronicle Books, 1989.

Gordon, Sarah H. *Passage to Union: How the Railroads Transformed American Life, 1829–1929*. Chicago: Ivan R. Dee, 1996.

Hawley, Samuel. *The Fight that Started the Movies: The World Heavyweight Championship, the Birth of the Cinema and the First Feature Film*. N.p.: Conquistador Press, 2016.

Hirsch, Susan E., and Robert I. Goler. *A City Comes of Age: Chicago in the 1890s*. Chicago: Chicago Historical Society, 1990.

Hunt, Donna Hord. *Frontier Denison, Texas*. Denison, TX: privately published, 2015.

Hunt, Donna Hord, and Mavis Anne Bryant. *Denison*. Images of America. Charleston, SC: Arcadia Publishing, 2011.

Jensen, Oliver. *The American Heritage History of Railroads in America*. Reprint, New York: Bonanza Books, 1981. Originally published in 1975.

Kasson, Joy S. *Buffalo Bill's Wild West: Celebrity, Memory, and Popular History*. New York: Hill and Wang, 2000.

Kelly, Dayton. *The Handbook of Waco and McLennan County, Texas*. Waco, TX: Texian Press, 1972.

Larson, Erik. *The Devil in the White City: Murder, Magic, and Madness at the Fair that Changed America*. New York: Vintage Books, 2003.

Masterson, Vincent Victor. *The Katy Railroad and the Last Frontier*. Norman: University of Oklahoma Press,1953.

Matthews, Kenneth, and Robert McDevitt. *The Unlikely Legacy: The Story of John Ringling, the Circus and Sarasota*. Sarasota, FL: Aaron Publishers Inc., 1980.

McCall, John, and Frank Scultz III. *Katy Southwest: Steam and Diesel Power Pictorial*. Dallas, TX: Kachina Press, 1985.

Memorial and Biographical History of McLennan, Falls, Bell and Coryell Counties. Chicago: Lewis Publishing Company, 1893.

Ogburn, Charlton. *Railroads: The Great American Adventure*. Washington, D.C.: National Geographic Society, 1977.

Phillips, Lance. *Yonder Comes the Train*. New York: A.S. Barnes & Company, 1965; second printing, 1967.

Philpott, William Albert. *Cinder in Your Eye and a Hodgepodge Miscellany, Including Jingle Fillers*. Dallas, TX: Egan Company, 1957.

Price, Lucie Clift. *Monuments of the Past: Letters of Maggie Dunn and William Henry Clift.* Austin, TX: privately published, 1976.

Reed, Robert O. *Train Wrecks: A Pictorial History of Accidents on the Main Line.* New York: Bonanza Books, 1968.

Reinhardt, Richard, ed. *Workin' on the Railroad: Reminiscences from the Age of Steam.* Palo Alto, CA: American West Publishing Company, 1970.

Reisdorff, James J. *The Man Who Wrecked 146 Locomotives: The Story of "Head-On Joe" Connolly.* Newton, KS: South Platte Press, 2009.

Schmidt, F.A. *Train Wrecks for Fun and Profit.* Erin, Ontario: Boston Mills Press,1982.

Stephens, A. Ray. *Historical Atlas of Texas.* Norman: University of Oklahoma Press, 2010, 241.

Stover, John F. *American Railroads.* Chicago: University of Chicago Press, 1961, 1997.

Turner, Decherd, ed. *That's All for Today: Selected Writings of Tom Gooch.* Dallas, TX: Southern Methodist University Press, 1955.

Waco, Texas City Directory, 1917, U.S. City Directories. https://www.ancestry.com.

Wallace, Patricia Ward. *Waco: Texas Crossroads.* Woodland Hills, CA: Windsor Publications, 1983.

White, Richard. *Railroaded: The Transcontinentals and the Making of Modern America.* New York: W.W. Norton & Company, 2011.

Who's Who in Railroading in North America. New York: Simmons-Boardman Publishing Corporation, 1930.

Wolmar, Christian. *The Great Railroad Revolution: The History of Trains in America.* New York: Public Affairs, 2012.

Monographs

Conger, Roger. *Crash at Crush: Famous Duel of the Iron Monsters.* Waco, TX: Texian Press, 1960.

Fundamentals of the Steam Locomotive. Omaha, NE: Rail Heritage Publications, 1949, 1983.

Jones, Lloyd W. *Humor Along the Katy Lines.* Dallas, TX: Southwest Railroad Historical Society Inc., 1970.

Missouri-Kansas-Texas Railroad. *The Opening of the Great Southwest: A Brief History of the Origin and Development of the Missouri-Kansas-Texas Railroad, Better Known as the KATY.* Dallas, TX: MKT Railroad, 1970.

Magazines

Barnes, Frank. "The Last Survivor." *Railroad Magazine* (May 1967).
———. "Train Wreck." *True West* (May–June 1957): 14–17.
Boissoneault, Lorraine. "A Train Company Crashed Two Trains. You Will Believe What Happened Next." July 28, 2017. Smithsonian.com.
Chilton, Stuart. "Train Wreck on Purpose." *Houston Chronicle Rotogravure Magazine* (August 19, 1956).
Connolly, "Head-On" Joe. "I Wrecked 146 Locomotives." *Railroad Stories* (April 1933).
Cross, Howard. "Great Train Wreck." *Katy Flyer* (July 1978).
Davis, Laura Smalley. "Katy's Crash." *The Cattleman* (June 1964): 72, 74.
Hamilton, Allen Lee. "Train Crash at Crush." *American West* (July–August 1983).
Hofsommer, Don L. "The Great Crash at Crush." *Trains Magazine* (September 1977): 30–31.
Katy Flyer. "Head-On Train Collision Stunt." (September 1996): 7–8.
Kent, Alan. "Death Duel of the Iron Monsters." *Parade* (October 1977): 24–25.
Medallion. "Tex-Czechs: Slavic Immigrants Transformed Culture of Central Texas" (May–June 2008): 8–11. Texas Historical Commission.
MKT Employee Magazine. "W.G. Crush Did Much in 40 Years to Increase Katy's Popularity" (January 1934): 8–9.
Norton, Paul. "Train Wrecks Made to Order." *Railway Progress* (May 1953): 24–30.
Peeler, Tom. "Retro: A Smashing Idea." *D Magazine* (December 1989).
Phelan, Richard. "Yesterday: The Fighters on This Card Stoked Their Fires and Came Out Steaming." *Sports Illustrated* (March 21, 1983).
Pitts, Jerry. "William Crush's Smashing Idea." *Katy Flyer* (September 1996): 3–6.
Railway Agent and Station Agent. "The Courteous and Gentlemanly G.P.A." (January 1891): 202.
Rogers, Austin. "A Pre-Arranged Head End Collision." *Cosmopolitan* (December 1896): 125–29.
Sanders, J.R. "Crush's Locomotive Crash Was a Monster Smash." *Wild West* (April 2010).
Scribner's Monthly 6, no. 3. "The Great South: The New Route to the Gulf" (July 1873): 257–88.
Swartz, Clay. "The Crash at Crush." *Cowboys & Indians* (August–September 2014): 114–18.
Waco Heritage & History 8, no. 3 (Fall 1977). Waco Historical Society.

NEWSPAPERS

Akron (OH) Beacon Journal
Alton (IL) Telegraph
Austin American-Statesman
Austin Daily Statesman
Boston Herald
Canton (OH) Repository
Chicago Inter Ocean
Chicago Tribune
(Columbus) Ohio State Journal
Dallas Morning News
Dallas Times-Herald
Denison Herald
Denison Sunday Gazetteer
Des Moines (IA) Daily News
Fort Scott (KS) Daily Monitor
Fort Worth Gazette
Fort Worth Star-Telegram
Galveston Daily News
Houston Chronicle
Houston Post

Lancaster (OH) Daily Eagle
Louisville (KY) Courier-Journal
Marion (OH) Star
Marshall (TX) News Messenger
New York World
Parsons (KS) Daily Sun
Salt Lake (UT) Tribune
San Antonio Express
San Antonio Express-News
San Antonio Light
Sedalia (MO) Democrat
Shiner (TX) Gazette
St. Louis Post-Dispatch
St. Louis Republic
St. Paul (MN) Globe
Temple Times
Waco Tribune-Herald
Waco Weekly Tribune
West (TX) News

INDEX

ABOUT THE AUTHOR

An elected member of the Texas Institute of Letters, Mike Cox is the author of more than thirty nonfiction books. Over an award-winning freelance career dating back to his high school days, he has written hundreds of newspaper articles, columns, magazine stories and essays for a wide variety of regional and national publications. When not writing, he spends as much time as he can traveling, fishing, hunting and looking for new stories to tell. He lives in the Hill Country village of Wimberley, Texas. Weary of traffic jams in his nearby hometown of Austin, he's all for the development of high-speed passenger train service to lure people from their cars and SUVs.